DAI
READI
WITH
MARGARET SILF

Also by Margaret Silf

ଚ ୧ ଚ ୧

DAILY
READINGS

WITH

MARGARET SILF

DARTON · LONGMAN + TODD

First published in 2005 by
Darton, Longman and Todd Ltd
1 Spencer Court
140–142 Wandsworth High Street
London SW18 4JJ

Material selected from *Daysprings*,
first published in 2001 by Darton, Longman and Todd.

ISBN 0 232 52631 1

A catalogue record for this book is available from
the British Library.

Designed and produced by Sandie Boccacci
Set in 11.5/14pt Bembo
Printed and bound in Great Britain by
The Cromwell Press, Trowbridge, Wiltshire

Contents

❧ v ❧

Introduction

Have you ever enjoyed a fondue? Have you ever dipped a piece of bread into a bowl of bubbling melted cheese, or a ripe strawberry into a pot of silky warm chocolate? If so, you'll know that what is apparently very ordinary can be transformed into something rather *extra*-ordinary by dipping it into the right substance.

I hope it isn't stretching imagination too far to suggest that God is a bit like a fondue. When our ordinary experiences are 'dipped in God', they can become extra-ordinary. When we ourselves – our hearts and minds – are dipped in God, then we too can be transformed.

We don't have to be saints or mystics to be dipped in God. We can experience God's fondue just by taking a few minutes each day to dip into the wisdom of scripture, and let the spirit of what we find there soak into the happenings and circumstances of our everyday living.

This little book of reflections invites you to do that. Each day offers you a short reading from scripture and a bite-sized reflection on it. These 'bites' are my own selection of what I liked best from the fuller, lectionary-based book first published by DLT under the title *Daysprings*. May you discover your own connections, as you ponder.

I wish you the joy of a journey through the year with God, and may the events and encounters of every day, whether of joy or frustration, take on the flavour and the meaning of the One who is with you in and through them all.

Thank you ...

To the people of North Staffordshire, for whom
the original reflections in *Daysprings* were
written, as weekly leaflets called *Potter's Clay*,
and to Brendan Walsh and Helen Porter at DLT
for suggesting, and bringing to birth, this new
'daughter of *Daysprings*'.

JANUARY

January 1st

May the Lord bless you and keep you.
May the Lord let his face shine on you
and be gracious to you.
May the Lord uncover his face to you
and bring you peace.

(Numbers 6:24–26)

A new year and another mile of the journey. Three hundred and sixty-five new chances to watch the sun rise on God's surprises along the way. Three hundred and sixty-five windows of opportunity through which to glimpse the face of God in the rock face of everyday life.

January 2nd

*You are anointed with truth, not with a lie,
and as it has taught you, so you must stay
in him. Live in Christ.*

(1 John 2:27)

The touch of your truth on our hearts is the reason why every falsehood within us leaves us feeling exiled from our real home in you. It is the touchstone that warns us when we are allowing something less than the best in us to determine what we say and do.

January 3rd

My dear people, we are already the children of God
but what we are to be in the future has not yet been
revealed; all we know is that when it is revealed,
we shall be like him, because we shall see him
as he really is.

(1 John 3:2)

The first week of the holiday passed by in disappointing
dullness. The mountains were shrouded in fog and a
penetrating drizzle soaked into the valleys. They might as
well have stayed at the airport, for all they could see of the
countryside. Then one morning the clouds broke and a
clear day dawned. They gasped with delight as the whole
splendour of the Alpine range was suddenly there, spread
out before their eyes. It had always been there, of course,
but now they could see it as it really was.

January 4th

As John stood there with two of his disciples, Jesus passed, and John stared hard at him and said, 'Look, there is the lamb of God.' Hearing this, the two disciples followed Jesus. Jesus turned round, saw them and said 'What do you want?' They answered, 'Rabbi' – which means Teacher – 'Where do you live?' 'Come and see,' he replied.

(John 1:35–39)

Maureen struggled to make sense of her science book with its diagrams of seeds and trees and flowers. In her six short years she had never been out of the city, never seen a field or a forest. Then the school trip came round. The bus took them far away into a world they hadn't even begun to imagine. The teacher took Maureen's hand. 'Come and see the acorns, Maureen, and the oak trees. Come and see how they *really* are.'

*Philip found Nathaniel and told him, 'We have found
the One Moses wrote about in the Law, the One
about whom the prophets wrote. He is Jesus son of
Joseph, from Nazareth.' 'From Nazareth?' said
Nathaniel, 'Can anything good come out of that
place?' 'Come and see,' replied Philip.*

(John 1:45–46)

We would never refuse to unwrap a gift because we don't
like the colour of the wrapping paper. Why, then, do we
so often refuse to get to know our neighbours, for no
better reason?

January 6th

Going into the house they saw the child with his
mother Mary, and falling to their knees they did him
homage. Then, opening their treasures, they offered him
gifts of gold, frankincense and myrrh.

(Matthew 2:11)

Carol paused for a moment and rested her hand on the head of her small son, sleeping in the little bed. As she did so, she remembered the day. There had been a shaft of gold, when his laughter had broken through the greyness of her anxiety. There had been a moment of true prayer, when he had held his breath in delight as a robin hopped across the window-sill. There had been a time of pain and its healing, as she had soothed his grazed knee and kissed away his tears. Gold for joy; incense for prayer; myrrh for healing. Gifts from a child. Gifts for a Child.

January 7th

Jesus took the five loaves and the two fish, raised his eyes to heaven and said the blessing; then he broke the loaves and handed them to his disciples to distribute among the people. He also shared out the two fish among them all.

(Mark 6:41)

We may prepare the food with care and express our thanks to you in all sincerity, but until we share it with our brothers and sisters, the meal has no meaning and the miracle no power.

January 8th

Jesus spoke to them, and said: 'Courage! It is I!
Do not be afraid!' Then he got into the boat
with them, and the wind dropped.

(Mark 6:50–51)

You calm our life's storms, not by changing our circumstances, but by entering into them with us and changing
our fear into trust.

January 9th

*A man who does not love the brother that he can see
cannot love God, whom he has never seen.*

(1 John 4:20)

My heart may melt with compassion when I see the plight
of refugees on the other side of the world, but if I can't
find the time to attend to the needs of the people next
door, I am failing to live in love.

January 10th

You do not ask for sacrifice and offerings,
but an open ear.
You do not ask for holocaust and victim.
Instead, here am I.

(Psalm 39:6–7)

Emily was the envy of her classmates. She had everything a teenager could wish for. Her parents worked from morning till night to buy her all she could desire. Jenny had nothing – except a Mum and Dad who were there for her and listened to her dreams.

January 11th

Unrolling the scroll he found the place where it is written: 'The spirit of the Lord has been given to me, for he has anointed me. He has sent me to bring the good news to the poor, to proclaim liberty to captives and to the blind new sight, to set the downtrodden free, to proclaim the Lord's year of favour' ... Then he began to speak to them: 'This text is being fulfilled even as you listen.'

(Luke 4:17–22)

For two thousand years we have waited for your Coming, and every day we have missed it, because we were expecting it tomorrow.

January 12th

Jesus' reputation continued to grow, and large crowds
would gather to hear him and to have their sickness
cured, but he would always go off to some place where
he could be alone and pray.

(Luke 5:15–16)

When I need you most, Lord, you sometimes seem so far
away. It is then, perhaps, that you are in your lonely place,
drawing from your Father the strength for both of us.

January 13th

*As Jesus was walking along by the Sea of Galilee
he saw Simon and his brother Andrew casting a net
in the lake – for they were fishermen. And Jesus
said to them, 'Follow me and I will make you
into fishers of men.'*

(Mark 1:16–18)

Every loving relationship I form with those I meet is a
thread in the net you are weaving, with which to draw
your people home. Let me be sure to keep them all in
good repair.

January 14th

*Ruth said to Naomi: 'Do not press me to leave you
and to turn back from your company, for "wherever
you go, I will go, wherever you live, I will live,
your people shall be my people and your God,
my God".'*

(Ruth 1:3–6)

If we wear a disciple's sandals, they may lead us where we
would rather not walk, alongside people we would rather
not know. If your Father is our Father, too, then your ways
shall be ours.

January 15th

'I tell you that many will come from east and west to take their places with Abraham and Isaac and Jacob at the feast in the kingdom of heaven.'

(Matthew 8:11)

The dinner guests were carefully screened to avoid social discomfort. The conversation was suitably polite and the atmosphere a little chilled. Down the road at the hostel the men shivered as they wrapped thankful hands round bowls of hot soup; friendly banter warmed up the raw night air. It was a feast, because love sat among them.

January 16th

The Lord said to Samuel, 'Take no notice of his appearance or his height for I have rejected him; God does not see as man sees; man looks at appearances but the Lord looks at the heart.'

(1 Samuel 16:7)

Marjorie took home a bouquet of the most expensive blooms from the flower show. Christine bought herself a dozen daffodil bulbs. The appearance is for today, but the heart belongs to tomorrow.

Jesus went into the synagogue, and there was a man there who had a withered hand ... Jesus said to the man, 'Stretch out your hand.' He stretched it out and his hand was better.

(Mark 3:1, 5)

When I'm feeling low I nurse my sorrows like a broken arm, and wrap myself in self-pity. I only know of one cure: to stretch out my hands and my heart towards another person who is feeling worse.

January 18th

The word of God is something alive and active;
it cuts like any double-edged sword, but more finely.

(Hebrews 4:12)

The two-edged blade of your Spirit slices through my being, Lord, like the blade of a master sculptor, ruthlessly stripping me of all that hinders my growth in you, yet tenderly revealing the shape and form of who I really am.

January 19th

*Jesus said to his disciples, 'I tell you solemnly, it will
be hard for a rich man to enter the kingdom of
heaven. Yes, I tell you again, it is easier for a camel
to pass through the eye of a needle than for a
rich man to enter the kingdom of heaven.'*

(Matthew 19:23–24)

The climbers had to leave their rucksacks behind, before
attempting the summit. The most beautiful and mysterious
places of the mountain were only accessible through the
slimmest of openings between the rocks, where there was
no room for any baggage.

January 20th

Jesus went home, and such a crowd collected that they could not even have a meal. When his relatives heard of this they set out to take charge of him, convinced he was out of his mind.

(Mark 3:20–21)

A goldfinch strayed into the garden one day. The sparrows were bewildered. Their bewilderment turned to hostility. They turned against the goldfinch and drove him away, for the ordinary cannot tolerate for long the presence of the extraordinary.

January 21st

The people that walked in darkness
has seen a great light;
on those who live in a land of deep shadow
a light has shone.

(Isaiah 9:1)

When I turn my back on the Light of my life, I see only
the darkness of my own shadow; but I only need to turn,
and the shadow will be behind me.

January 22nd

Shepherds ought to feed their flock, yet you have fed
on milk, you have dressed yourselves in wool, you
have sacrificed the fattest sheep, but failed to feed the
flock. You have failed to make weak sheep strong, or to
care for the sick ones, or bandage the wounded ones.

(Ezekiel 34:3–4)

Forgive us, Lord, for we have shorn you of your wool, and
not even bound the wounds of that shearing. We have
drained you of your milk, yet failed to nourish you for its
replenishing. We have done this to our brothers and sisters,
Lord. We have done it to you.

January 23rd

*Jesus replied: 'Who are my mother and my brothers?'
And looking round at those sitting in a circle about
him, he said, 'Here are my mother and my brothers.
Anyone who does the will of God, that person is my
brother and sister and mother.'*

(Mark 3:33–35)

We belong to the biggest family on earth. We are responsible for the loving-care of a million siblings, and they for us. In our kinship with each other, our loneliness ends, but our responsibility begins.

January 24th

The Spirit of the Lord set me down in the middle of a
valley, a valley full of bones … He said, 'Dry bones,
hear the word of the Lord. The Lord says this to the
bones. "I am now going to make the breath enter you,
and you will live. I shall put sinews on you, I shall
make flesh grow on you. I shall cover you with skin
and give you breath, and you will live; and you will
learn that I am the Lord."'

(Ezekiel 37:1–7)

Hannah was numbed with grief after her life companion
died. She sat, day after day, gazing at faded photographs of
their childhood and their youth, immobilised by sadness
and regret. Until one day the neighbour's little girl
knocked on her door, with a message from her parents. It
was the start of a new friendship. The old lady and the
child would sit and chat together, until Hannah's faded
photographs became a new, living love.

January 25th

I will not enter the house where I live
nor go to the bed where I rest.
I will give no sleep to my eyes,
to my eyelids will give no slumber
till I find a place for the Lord.

(Psalm 132:3–5)

A day that passes without contact with you is a day when I feel exiled from my innermost home; a night that I enter without seeking your blessing is a night without my deepest rest.

January 26th

This is what the kingdom of God is like. A man throws seed on the land. Night and day, while he sleeps, when he is awake, the seed is sprouting and growing; how, he does not know. Of its own accord the land produces first the shoot, then the ear, then the full grain in the ear.

(Mark 4:26–29)

Nothing can prevent the secret, silent growth of your seed in our hearts, unless we cover it over and flatten it down with the weight of our own imagined wisdom.

January 27th

*David's anger flared up against the man [who had
stolen the poor man's ewe lamb]. 'As the Lord lives,'
he said to Nathan, 'the man who did this deserves to
die! He must make fourfold restitution for the lamb,
for doing such a thing and showing no compassion.'
Then Nathan said to David, 'You are the man.'*

(2 Samuel 12:57)

It had been a heavy day in court for Justice John: several
cases of benefit fraud, a couple of car thefts and a man who
had fiddled his expense claims. 'They had it coming to
them,' he thought to himself, complacently, as he picked
up his phone and called his stockbroker. With his privi-
leged inside knowledge about the coming takeover bid,
now was the right moment to make a killing on those
share dealings.

January 28th

How happy are the poor in spirit;
theirs is the kingdom of heaven.

(Matthew 5:3)

Susie watched delightedly as the soap bubbles rose into the air. When she tried to clasp and possess them with her small, eager hands, they burst and vanished. But when she made no claim on them and let them float freely, they reflected all the colours of the rainbow back into her shining eyes.

January 29th

A man with an unclean spirit came out from the
tombs towards Jesus. The man lived in the tombs and
no-one could secure him any more, even with a chain,
because he had often been secured with fetters and
chains but had snapped the chains and broken the
fetters, and no-one had the strength to control him.

(Mark 5:2–5)

There are parts of me that I have buried so deeply that
even *I* can no longer recognise them. There are aspects of
my personality that I keep firmly fastened down with the
chains of all my energy, for fear of what they might do
if they broke loose. But when the volcano erupts, and
the chains snap and my very worst breaks out, I find
you standing there, to recognise, to heal, and to lead me
to freedom.

January 30th

Mercy and faithfulness have met;
justice and peace have embraced.

(Psalm 85:10)

Greg's son was blinded in the terrorist attack. His outraged sense of justice demanded retaliation, but his son's new vision saw things differently. 'They are blinder than I am, Dad,' he said quietly. 'Don't let them blind you, too.'

January 31st

*I shall give you a new heart, and put a new spirit in
you; I shall remove the heart of stone from your bodies
and give you a heart of flesh instead.*

(Ezekiel 36:26–27)

We seek to by-pass our hearts with all the defences and
delusions we can muster. Give us the courage to surrender
ourselves instead to your transplant operation.

FEBRUARY

All these [Abraham, Sarah, Isaac, Jacob] died in faith,
before receiving any of the things that had been
promised, but they saw them in the far distance and
welcomed them, recognising that they were only
strangers and nomads on earth.

(Hebrews 11:13)

Mother Teresa has not abolished poverty, nor did Anne Frank set her people free. But their journeys in trust, towards the distant star of truth and love, have carried the whole human family with them.

February 2nd

'Now, Master, you can let your servant go in peace,
just as you promised,
because my eyes have seen the salvation
which you have prepared for all the nations to see,
a light to enlighten the pagans
and the glory of your people Israel.'

(Luke 2:29–32)

When you kindle your light in our hearts, you kindle it not so that we might remain comfortably in its warm glow, but so that we might go forward in your peace, carrying light into the waiting darkness.

February 3rd

*'What is your name?' Jesus asked the Gerasene
demoniac. 'My name is legion,' he answered, 'for there
are many of us.'*

(Mark 5:9)

Adam is known by many names: his children call him
'Dad' and his pupils call him 'Sir'; his friends call him
generous and his family call him extravagant; he calls himself angry, and tender, and frightened and bold, confused
and confident; he changes his names as often as he changes
his mood. His true name, the name of his wholeness, is
only known to *you*.

February 4th

'You are the salt of the earth. But if the salt becomes tasteless, what can make it salty again? It is good for nothing, and can only be thrown out to be trampled underfoot by men.'

(Matthew 5:13)

The salt of our earth comes in fine silver salt cellars, for the seasoning of our food; but it also comes in bins at the road-side, for the thawing of snow and ice. We are called to awaken in those around us the appetite for God, and to melt away the barriers that hold them back.

February 5th

Then Simon Peter spoke up: 'You are the Christ,' he said, 'the Son of the living God.' Jesus replied 'Simon, son of Jonah, you are a happy man; because it was not flesh and blood that revealed this to you but my Father in heaven.'

(Matthew 16:15–17)

We spend years of our lives gathering knowledge and understanding from our learning and experience, but the inner certainties of true wisdom come to us, unbidden, in timeless moments of revealed clarity.

February 6th

Yet will God really live with men on the earth? Why,
the heavens and their own heavens cannot contain
you. How much less this house that I have built.

(1 Kings 8:27–28)

It may take a lifetime to clear space in our hearts for
God; and can such space contain him? Only if it is big
enough to contain the smallest and most insignificant of
his creatures.

February 7th

Continue to love each other like brothers, and remember always to welcome strangers, for by doing this, some people have entertained angels without knowing it.

(Hebrews 13:1–2)

If we receive everyone who crosses our threshold as if they were an angel, we might be surprised to find how many of them *react* as if they were.

February 8th

They even offered their own sons
and their daughters in sacrifice to demons,
till his anger blazed against his people:
he was filled with horror at his chosen ones.

(Psalm 106:36–40)

David saw no connection between his worries about his teenage daughter's casual attitude towards her relationship with her boyfriend, and the 'adult' magazines he carried in his own briefcase.

February 9th

Lying in bed I wonder, 'When will it be day?'
Risen I think, 'How slowly evening comes!'
Restlessly I fret till twilight falls.

(Job 7:4)

My thoughts and fears stretch me out into an unknown tomorrow, and I live my life in the tension of a taut elastic band, unless I can let go my hold, and relax into the peace that only the *present* moment can ever offer.

February 10th

'How many loaves have you?' 'Seven,' they said.
Then he instructed the crowd to sit down on the
ground, and he took the seven loaves, and after giving
thanks he broke them and handed them to his
disciples to distribute, and they distributed them
among the crowd ... Now there had been about
four thousand people.

(Mark 8:5–6, 9)

The logic of the Lord is simple. The little we have must be divided, before it can be multiplied. The things we cling to must be taken away, before the fullness of his love can be added to our own.

February 11th

*A man on his way abroad summoned his servants and
entrusted his property to them. To one he gave five
talents, to another two, to a third, one; each in
proportion to his ability. Then he set out. The man
who had received the five talents promptly went and
traded with them and made five more. The man who
had received two made two more in the same way. But
the man who had received one went off and dug a
hole in the ground and hid his master's money.*

(Matthew 25:14–18)

Alice had been looking forward so much to seeing her
grandsons again. She noticed straight away that they were
wearing the sweaters she had knitted for them last year.
John's was getting thin and worn. It had received its share
of life's batterings and hugs. Her heart rejoiced. But Jim's
looked as smart as on the day she had given it to him.
Barely worn, she thought. And her heart sank.

February 12th

And for anyone who is in Christ, there is a new
creation; the old creation has gone, and now the new
one is here.

(2 Corinthians 5:17–18)

Peter's hobby is wood-turning. He can pick up a piece of
rough timber from the wood-yard and know, with his
fingertips, the new thing that his skill can draw out of it.
He has a vision of the grain and the colour and the shape
which only his heart's eyes can see, as he clamps the block
to the lathe. Would that he could realise that what he does
for the wood, you are doing for him.

February 13th

God called to him from the middle of the bush.
'Moses, Moses!' he said. 'Here I am,' he answered.
'Come no nearer,' he said. 'Take off your shoes, for the
place on which you stand is holy ground.'

(Exodus 3:4–5)

When heart speaks to heart, and another human being confides to you something of the deepest things that touch him or concern her, go barefoot and respect the sacred space that lies open and revealed between you. For you stand on holy ground.

February 14th

Love is always patient and kind; love is never jealous;
love is not boastful or conceited, it is never rude and
never seeks its own advantage, it does not take offence
or store up grievances. Love does not rejoice at wrong-
doing, but finds its joy in the truth. It is always ready
to make allowances, to trust, to hope and to endure
whatever comes.

(1 Corinthians 13:4–7)

We try to gift-wrap our loving in the pink ribbons of our transient emotions. But love is not an emotion. Love is a decision. A decision to choose, in every situation, the more loving response.

February 15th

When the Lord comes he will light up all that is
hidden in the dark and reveal the secret intentions
of men's hearts.

(1 Corinthians 4:5)

If we could see each others' hearts as God sees us, we
might be surprised to see what selfish motives sometimes
prompt our generosity, and what love is often buried
underneath our worst mistakes.

February 16th

*A body dies when it is separated from the spirit, and
in the same way faith is dead if it is separated from
good deeds.*

(James 2:26)

Nancy's houseplants died while she was in hospital. And
inwardly she died, too, when there was no message or
greeting from Julie, her daughter. The third death that day
was Julie's, who could have watered Nancy's heart with a
few drops of love, but didn't.

February 17th

Once we put a bit into the horse's mouth, to make it do what we want, we have the whole animal under our control. Or think of ships, no matter how big they are, even if a gale is driving them, the man at the helm can steer them anywhere he likes by controlling a tiny rudder.

(James 3:3–5)

If I trust you for my rudder, the whole unwieldy bulk of my wayward heart can be guided by your gentlest touch. If I rely on my own steering I will spend all my life's energy and fail to change my course by even a fraction.

February 18th

Didn't you realise that you were God's temple and that the Spirit of God was living among you? If anybody should destroy the temple of God, God will destroy him, because the temple of God is sacred and you are that temple.

(1 Corinthians 3:16–17)

Christine had angel's hands, the doctors used to say. No-one knew quite why she was so much finer a nurse than her colleagues. They all treated their charges as fellow human beings. Except Christine. She handled every patient as if she were touching God.

February 19th

*Stay awake, because you do not know the day when
your master is coming.*

(Matthew 24:42)

Not with the anxious wakefulness of night we await you,
but with the eager wakefulness of dawning.

February 20th

*Where do these wars and battles between yourselves
first start? Isn't it precisely in the desires fighting
inside your own selves? You want something and you
haven't got it; so you are prepared to kill. You have an
ambition that you cannot satisfy; so you fight to get
your way by force.*

(James 4:1–2)

I switched on the television news, and saw my own inner
conflicts, writ large. I saw the inner struggles of every
member of the human family stamped onto a barren
battlefield and scarred indelibly across the faces of the
innocent. Then I switched off the television, and knew that
peace could only begin with me.

Have mercy on me, God, in your kindness,
In your compassion blot out my offence.
O wash me more and more from my guilt
and cleanse me from my sin.

(Psalm 51:1–2)

Eileen was helping her son with his packing to go off to
university. Among his clothes she noticed an old, worn
sweater with a faded dark stain. She remembered how he
had come home from school one day, with ink all over
him, how she had shouted at him, how he had cried, how
she had scrubbed and washed and rinsed it, week after
week, until the stain had faded, but never disappeared.
They looked at each other, over the pile of clothes. 'I
remember how you tried to get it out, Mum,' he said. 'But
I want it with me, not because you tried so hard to clean
it, but because you made it for me in the first place.'

February 22nd

*To everyone who has will be given more, and he will
have more than enough; but from the man who has
not, even what he has will be taken away.*

(Matthew 25:29)

The nudge of inspiration comes quietly, urging us to
exercise a hidden talent and let it bear fruit. If we respond,
it will grow, strengthening our confidence and ability. If we
ignore it, it will fade and be lost, and we may never know
what gifts we have left buried in the unexplored depths of
our lives.

February 23rd

In sacrifice you take no delight,
burnt offerings from me you would refuse,
my sacrifice, a contrite spirit,
A humbled, contrite heart you will not spurn.

(Psalm 51:16–17)

Julian had had an awful day at work. Everything looked black and hopeless. He was in no mood to be kind to his little boy that evening. His son went to bed, miserable and bewildered by his father's anger. And Julian himself felt worse than ever. As he went to bed, he left an envelope by his son's bedside, with a peace-offering of some extra pocket money in it. It was a way of saying: 'Sorry!' But it made the boy feel worse next morning, and even more confused. Things didn't come right between them until the next evening when Julian came home, and held his son in a silent, heartfelt hug, which told them both that all was understood, and forgiven.

February 24th

You will rebuild the ancient ruins,
build up on the old foundations.
You will be called 'Breach-mender',
'Restorer of ruined houses'.

(Isaiah 58:12)

'We'll soon have you as good as new,' the doctor smiled down at Alice after her hip replacement operation. She smiled back gratefully, already certain in her heart that in *your* hands she was being made better than new.

February 25th

'Man does not live on bread alone,
but on every word that comes from the mouth
of God.'

(Matthew 4:4)

If I had to live only on what I can see and touch, what would I do for light, for warmth, for air or for power? What would I do for love?

February 26th

Jesus caught sight of two boats close to the bank. The fishermen had gone out of them and were washing their nets ... And Jesus said to Simon, 'Do not be afraid; from now on it is people you will catch.'

(Luke 5:1–2, 10)

The love of God is caught, not taught, and we are called to be the source of the contagion.

'The Spirit of the Lord has been given to me,
for he has anointed me.
He has sent me to bring the good news to the poor,
to proclaim liberty to captives and to the
blind new sight,
to set the downtrodden free, to proclaim the
Lord's year of favour.'

(Luke 4:18–19)

When we share a word of love with the lonely; when we
take a trembling hand into our own; when we help a child
to solve a problem or intervene to curb a playground fight,
we are sharing your anointing, Lord, and letting your
Kingdom show.

February 28th

God saw their efforts to renounce their evil behaviour.
And God relented: he did not inflict on them the
disaster which he had threatened.

(Jonah 3:10)

Miriam was trembling with suppressed anger as she dismissed the class after challenging them about their selfish behaviour. Most of them walked past her, heads in the air, eyes defiant. But as Malcolm shuffled past, she noticed the tears gathering in his eyes. He looked up at her, distressed; her face softened into gentleness, and he read forgiveness in her gaze.

February 29th

It is not those who say to me 'Lord, Lord,' who will enter the kingdom of heaven, but the person who does the will of my Father in heaven.

(Matthew 7:21)

My prayer ended, so I thought, with a heartfelt promise to you to mend that strained relationship. The real prayer began when I saw her coming towards me in the street and faced up to my desire to avoid the meeting.

MARCH

March 1st

*'You have learnt how it was said to our ancestors: you
must not kill, and if anyone does kill he must answer
for it before the court. But I say this to you; anyone
who is angry with his brother will answer for it before
the court; if a man calls his brother "Fool" he will
answer for it before the Sanhedrin; and if a man calls
him "Renegade" he will answer for it in hell fire.'*

(Matthew 5:21–22)

I noticed how my angry retort had caused my colleague
to shrivel and shrink. And I realised, too late, that in the
warmth of a kinder and more generous word, she could
have grown and blossomed.

March 2nd

*'I set before you life or death, blessing or curse.
Choose Life!'*

(Deuteronomy 30:19)

Sinking behind the mountain of stress, we may glimpse a
beautiful sunset. Right at the heart of shabby supermarket
consumerism, eager, generous hands drop their contribu-
tions into the charity box. And a child's trusting smile
survives our grumblings. Little pointers, showing the
direction to Life.

March 3rd

*And now the life you have is hidden with Christ
in God. But when Christ is revealed – and he is
your life – you too will be revealed in all your
glory with him.*

(Colossians 3:3–4)

Our daffodil bulbs can have no idea of what they will
become next April. But we, who have planted them in the
darkness, we know what glory lies hidden in their hearts
and we rejoice in the joy and trust of anticipation.

March 4th

Cease to do evil,
learn to do good,
search for justice,
help the oppressed.

(Isaiah 1:16–17)

After the drink-driving conviction, Jim had to stop driving immediately. It took him rather longer to learn to live free of his addiction. And then, very gradually, to discover how to channel his energies into helping those people he had harmed.

March 5th

*One sabbath Jesus happened to be taking a walk
through the cornfields, and his disciples were picking
ears of corn, rubbing them in their hands and eating
them. Some of the Pharisees said: 'Why are you doing
something that is forbidden on the sabbath day?'
And he said to them, 'The Son of Man is
master of the sabbath.'*

(Luke 6:1–3, 5)

Forgive us, Lord, when the complications we impose upon
ourselves and on each other prevent us from simply living.

March 6th

'I was hungry, and you never gave me food ...'

(Matthew 25:42)

We heard that you were hungry and we called a conference to discuss food vouchers.

Father, forgive!

You looked lost in our neighbourhood, and we closed ranks.

Father, forgive!

You were dirty and dishevelled, and we complained that our new shoes were hurting.

Father, forgive!

There was a rumour that you might have AIDS, and we took our child away from your child's school.

Father, forgive!

We heard that you were in prison, and we decided that it was probably your own fault.

Father, forgive!

March 7th

*Jesus answered: 'Can you drink the cup that I am
going to drink?' They replied, 'We can.' 'Very well,'
he said, 'you shall drink my cup.'*

(Matthew 20:22)

Your cup has many flavours, Lord: the cup of loneliness;
the cup of fear; the cup of poverty; the cup of terror.
But always, because your lips have touched it, it is a cup
of blessing.

March 8th

Happy indeed is the man
who follows not the counsel of the wicked;
nor lingers in the way of sinners,
nor sits in the company of scorners,
but whose delight is the law of the Lord.

(Psalm 1:1–2)

It seemed churlish, at the time, when Jean kept refusing to stay with her friends while they watched the forbidden videos. She came close to losing their friendship, until they began to sense that she was the one person in their group to whom they could turn when the things they had seen on the screen started to take hold of their real lives.

March 9th

The Lord is close to the broken-hearted;
Those whose spirit is crushed, he will save.

(Psalm 34:18)

The March winds play havoc with the newly sprung daffodils. I bend to gather those that have been snapped off in the night, before their buds had a chance to open, and I bring them into the warmth and let them open up their beauty. And a gentle voice whispers in the wind: 'If you care enough to do this for them, how much more surely will I do the same for you?'

March 10th

'It was the stone rejected by the builders
that became the keystone.'

(Matthew 21:42)

Catherine was turned down in all her job applications, because of her debilitating handicap. Then her application for a disability allowance was rejected on the grounds that her handicap was not sufficiently debilitating. Trapped in this cycle, she turned to you. She learned to pray, until her whole life became a prayer, and many people came to her, seeking peace, and wisdom, and *you*.

March 11th

The Pharisees and the scribes complained: 'This man,'
they said, 'welcomes sinners and eats with them.'

(Luke 15:1)

We may learn to tolerate those who offend us, but you
show us how to *welcome* them. We may bring ourselves to
send them a sandwich, but you call us to seek them out
and share the table with them.

March 12th

Jesus said to his disciples: 'Ask, and it will be given to you; search, and you will find; knock, and the door will be opened to you.'

(Matthew 7:7)

He stands at the door of our hearts. He will stand there through all our long, cold winters, if he has to. He will stand there until we hear him knocking, in our heart's silence. Until we realise that the handle is on *our* side of the door.

March 13th

My soul is longing for the Lord,
more than watchmen for daybreak.

(Psalm 130:7)

The nights were long, as my mother lay dying. But then, at dawn, she would often fall into a fitful sleep. I listened each night for the first single bird call before the dawn chorus proper began, and I watched for the first flush of sunrise over the garden. And then I would go out for half an hour among the roses. We met there, among the roses, and you received all the sorrows and the longings of the night into your new-dawning love.

March 14th

He then came down with them and stopped at a piece
of level ground where there was a large gathering of
his disciples with a great crowd of people … and
everyone in the crowd was trying to touch him because
power came out of him that cured them all.

(Luke 6:17–19)

You do not call us to climb mountains in your name or to
stand on the pinnacles of achievement. Instead you invite
us to come down, humbly, to the level ground, where your
people wait and hope and trust. You invite us only to be
there, carrying you in our hearts, trusting in your healing
power, for us, and for all.

March 15th

My soul is thirsting for God,
the God of my life;
when can I enter and see the face of God?

(Psalm 42:2)

The whole being of the crocus was concentrated on its thirst for the food and water that was nourishing its hidden secret. All through the winter it pushed determinedly, blindly, towards its still unknown fulfilment, until, on a cold March morning, it spread its flower to the full glory of the springtime sunshine.

March 16th

'Give, and there will be gifts for you: a full measure,
pressed down, shaken together, and running over, will
be poured into your lap.'

(Luke 6:38)

Our containers are far too small for the fullness of grace.
We have two choices: either we turn aside from the supply
and settle for what we have; or we let it overflow, and flood
the world around us.

March 17th

To let the oppressed go free,
and break every yoke,
to share your bread with the hungry,
and shelter the homeless poor,
to clothe the man you see to be naked
and not to turn from your own kin.
Then will your light shine like the dawn
and your wound be quickly healed over.

(Isaiah 58:6–8)

The friendly greeting, the liberating smile, the shared meal, the unplanned hospitality, the sensitive word to the one whose hurt has been exposed, the patient listening to an elderly relative: we barely notice them, in the giving, but in the one who receives, a new light may be kindled, for the road ahead.

The Spirit drove Jesus out into the wilderness and he remained there for forty days, and was tempted by Satan. He was with the wild beasts, and the angels looked after him.

(Mark 1:12–15)

Coming closer to you will expose the worst in ourselves and in each other. Will our hearts, at their limits, break down in fear, or expand into a new level of trust?

March 19th

A blessing on the man who puts his trust in the Lord,
with the Lord for his hope.
He is like a tree by the waterside that thrusts
its roots to the stream:
When the heat comes it feels no alarm,
its foliage stays green;
It has no worries in a year of drought,
and never ceases to bear fruit.

(Jeremiah 17:7–8)

With every prayer, our roots reach deeper, searching for the ground water. With every act of kindness, our branches stretch a little further to the sky, become a little greener. Root and branch. Darkness and light. Praying and living. Our wholeness and our fullness.

March 20th

While he was still a long way off, his father saw him and was moved with pity. He ran to the boy, clasped him in his arms and kissed him tenderly.

(Luke 15:20)

They found the runaway teenager in Singapore. A row over a football match, and he had taken himself halfway across the world on his father's credit card. That's what you could *really* call a family row. Easy to imagine what we might have to say to the lad, if he were ours, when he dares to come back … and perhaps not too difficult, either, to imagine the surge of joy and the heartfelt welcome at the airport, when we receive him safely home.

March 21st

The Lord said to Moses, 'Take with you some of the elders of Israel and move on to the forefront of the people; take in your hand the staff with which you struck the river, and go. I shall be standing with you there on the rock, at Horeb. You must strike the rock, and water will flow from it for the people to drink.'

(Exodus 17:5–6)

The rock face of my most intractable difficulties can become the source of your healing, life-giving stream, but only if I can stand squarely in front of it and claim its riches.

March 22nd

O send forth your light and your truth;
let these be my guide.
Let them bring me to your holy mountain
to the place where you dwell.

(Psalm 43:3)

The winter sea was as black as the starless night, as I stood on the deck of the ferry. A map would be useless in such a place, I thought. Then, for a brief moment, the sweeping beam from a distant lighthouse cut through the darkness. We were still far away from the harbour, but the direction was clear.

March 23rd

*Jesus said to his disciples 'Do not imagine that I have
come to abolish the Law or the Prophets. I have come
not to abolish but to complete them. I tell you solemnly
till heaven and earth disappear, not one dot, not one
little stroke, shall disappear from the Law until its
purpose is achieved.'*

(Matthew 5:17–18)

For as long as the river flows, it must respect the limits of
its banks, if its stream is not to become a destroying flood.
This is the law of its journey, until the journey ends and it
is poured into the ocean, and the riverbanks have served
their purpose.

March 24th

'I say this to you, who are listening: Love your enemies, do good to those who hate you, bless those who curse you, pray for those who treat you badly.'

(Luke 6:27)

When I disarm my enemy with a smile, I achieve far more than when I arm myself with sarcasm and disdain. Something negative is prevented and reversed, and one little arrow of pain is rendered harmless.

March 25th

I will fall like dew on Israel.
He shall bloom like the lily,
and thrust out roots like the poplar,
his shoots will spread far.

(Hosea 14:6–7)

The short time of my morning prayer, and the peace it gives me, seems to evaporate into the bustle of the day, as rapidly as the dew disappears from the grass blades at sunrise. Yet its effects penetrate every moment of that day, nourishing its roots, and enabling its fruitfulness.

March 26th

Making a whip out of some cord, Jesus drove them all
out of the Temple, cattle and sheep as well, scattered
the money-changers' coins, knocked their tables over
and said to the pigeon-sellers, 'Take all this out of here
and stop turning my Father's house into a market!'

(John 2:13–25)

I have mortgaged my heart to the world's passing satisfactions and securities, and I can't keep up the repayments. Lord, please re-possess me!

March 27th

The people stayed there watching Jesus. As for the leaders, they jeered at him. 'He saved others,' they said, 'let him save himself if he is the Christ of God, the Chosen One.'

(Luke 23:35–36)

It was hard for Mark to imagine, as he watched his father dying in agonising pain and disfigurement, that he had lived out his life as a surgeon whose touch had saved so many others. Then the end came, and as the stricken doctor gave back his life-breath to God, his face relaxed into a peace beyond understanding. It was in that moment that Mark understood the difference between truly healing and merely curing.

March 28th

*'Everyone who comes to me and listens to my words
and acts on them is like the man who, when he built
his house, dug and dug deep, and laid the foundations
on rock; when the river was in flood it bore down on
that house but could not shake it, it was so well built.'*

(Luke 6:47–49)

The builders' estimate arrived. It seemed incredible that
the foundations of the house should cost such a high proportion of the total price. A bit of concrete and steel that
would never be seen again. And my own foundations,
Lord? That part of me that no-one sees except you. Will
they hold firm when my life-floods rise? Are they built on
the rock of you, or on the sand of me?

March 29th

*'Listen to my voice, then I will be your God and you
shall be my people. Follow right to the end the way
that I have marked out for you.'*

(Jeremiah 7:23)

The crest of every hill revealed another, higher, more distant peak ahead, and there seemed to be no end to the
track marked out by the irregular stone cairns. We were
frequently disheartened, but we knew that the cairns
pointed the way to the perfect view, the vision, at the end
of the journey.

March 30th

*'I will heal their disloyalty, I will love them with all
my heart, for my anger has turned from them. I will
fall like dew on Israel.'*

(Hosea 14:5–6)

Dew is gentle. Dew falls silently, while we sleep, softening
our hard crusts so that grace might penetrate our hearts.

March 31st

Let us set ourselves to know the Lord;
that he will come is as certain as the dawn,
he will come to us as showers come,
like spring rains watering the earth.

(Hosea 6:3)

Ever so gradually the frozen earth thaws and the furrows start to crumble. The March sun gleams pale, clouds race, rain soaks and softens, and the seeds awaken from their winter dreaming. Just as gradually, just as gently, just as surely, does the light and warmth of God's love awaken our heart-seeds and draw them into the new life of an eternal springtime.

APRIL

April 1st

This day was made by the Lord,
we rejoice and are glad.

(Psalm 118:24)

It was the worst day Jim had ever experienced. Every hour
had pitched him more deeply into despair. Nothing and
nobody seemed to be on his side. At bedtime his little
daughter came to say 'Goodnight', her eyes sad and
uncomprehending. Something in her gaze opened the
floodgates of his grief. The tears rose. He held the child
close. She had torn aside the veil of darkness and he had
caught a glimpse of starlight. It had become, after all, a day
with a crack in it, through which God's love might find
entrance.

April 2nd

And indeed, everybody who does wrong hates
the light and avoids it,
for fear his actions should be exposed;
but the man who lives by the truth comes out
into the light,
so that it may be plainly seen that what he does
is done in God.

(John 3:20–21)

When we find the courage to come out of the darkness
and face the truth about who we really are, we discover an
unexpected bonus: the light also reveals to us the hurts and
needs of our sisters and brothers.

April 3rd

*Everything that is now covered will be uncovered, and
everything now hidden will be made clear. Whatever
you have said in the dark will be heard in the
daylight, and what you have whispered in hidden
places will be proclaimed on the housetops.*

(Luke 12:2, 3)

The paradox of your grace turns us inside out, until our
trembling, sin-stained hearts are fully exposed to the light
of your healing, all-revealing love.

April 4th

*Looking up, Jesus saw the crowds approaching and
said to Philip: 'Where can we buy some bread for
these people to eat?' ... Philip answered, 'Two
hundred denarii would only buy enough to give them
a small piece each.' One of his disciples, Andrew,
Simon Peter's brother, said, 'There is a small boy here
with five barley loaves and two small fish, but what is
that among so many?'*

(John 6:5–9)

Our 'much' provides almost nothing. Your 'almost nothing'
provides a feast.

April 5th

It was getting dark by now and Jesus had still not rejoined them. The wind was strong and the sea was getting rough. They had rowed three or four miles when they saw Jesus walking on the lake and coming towards the boat. This frightened them, but he said: 'It is I. Do not be afraid.' They were for taking him into the boat, but in no time it reached the shore at the place they were making for.

(John 6:17–21)

In our need, we are so concerned to bring you on board our little boat, that we forget that you hold all the power of the oceans in your hands.

April 6th

*He who is born of the earth
is earthly himself and speaks in an earthly way.
He who comes from heaven
bears witness to the things he has seen and heard.*

(John 3:31)

I come to you in prayer with mud on my feet, bringing my earth-self and my earth-bound hopes and needs. You send me back to earth with a grain of heaven in my heart, to be sown back into the earth of my today.

April 7th

*For God sent his Son into the world, not to condemn
the world, but so that through him the world
might be saved.*

(John 3:17)

You are not waiting to judge us for our failures in loving.
You are waiting to fill us with your own capacity to love.

April 8th

Do not work for food that cannot last,
but work for food that endures to eternal life.

(John 6:27)

I stopped beside a colleague's desk, and noticed the photographs of his two children propped up proudly against his files. 'That's to remind me why I'm really here,' he told me. 'When I'm tempted to pack it all in, I look at them and I know I'm working for something much more precious than a salary.' And I knew that my colleague was working for hope, working for love.

April 9th

They said to Jesus: 'What sign will you give to show us that we should believe in you? What work will you do? Our fathers had manna to eat in the desert.'

(John 6:30–31)

'Prove that you love me,' he said to her. 'Do what *I* want.' It was the end of their friendship. She found someone to whom she could *give* her love, where it was not demanded.

April 10th

'No-one can come to me
unless he is drawn by the Father who sent me.'

(John 6:44)

Jake tipped the iron filings out onto the sheet of paper, as the science teacher had told him to do. They lay there, quite lifeless and pointless. Then he gently drew the magnet across the paper and watched as they all moved towards the power so much greater than themselves, following the deepest laws of their nature.

April 11th

After this, many of his disciples left him and stopped
going with him … Then Jesus said to the Twelve,
'What about you, do you want to go away too?'
Simon Peter answered, 'Lord, who shall we go to? You
have the message of eternal life, and we believe; we
know that you are the Holy One of God.'

(John 6:66–68)

Once we have met ourselves, in you, stripped of all our
masks and our defences, there can be no way back. To turn
away again would be to violate the very heart of our
own reality.

April 12th

*Jesus went out into the hills to pray; and he spent the
whole night in prayer to God. When day came he
summoned his disciples and picked out twelve of
them; he called them 'apostles'.*

(Luke 6:12–13)

If every moment of decision were preceded by a night of
prayer, how differently our lives might run – if every daylight choice were shaped by your presence in our darkness.

April 13th

'Be compassionate as your Father is compassionate.
Do not judge, and you will not be judged yourselves;
do not condemn, and you will not be condemned;
grant pardon, and you will be pardoned.'

(Luke 6:36–37)

Karen used to criticise every other driver on the road, until one day her small son said: 'But *you* do that too, Mum.' It was a moment of truth and the remarkable thing was that when she stopped criticising others she had more energy to concentrate on being a better driver herself.

April 14th

Now while he was with them at table, he took the
bread and said the blessing; then he broke it and
handed it to them. And then their eyes were opened
and they recognised him.

(Luke 24:30–31)

Out of all the anguish and the turbulence of our present
moment and our present struggles, a familiar gesture,
instantly recognised, slices through the confusion with a
brilliant shaft of light. Moments of clarity, restoring our
certainty that your presence, like the sun, is always there,
and only the clouds come and go.

April 15th

The blessing-cup that we bless is a communion with the blood of Christ, and the bread that we break is a communion with the body of Christ. The fact that there is only one loaf means that, though there are many of us, we form a single body because we all have a share in this one loaf.

(1 Corinthians 10:15–17)

Our bread is consecrated only when we share it with our neighbour. Our cup is blessed only when we pass it on.

April 16th

'They have taken the Lord out of the tomb,' she said,
'and we don't know where they have put him.'

(John 20:2)

We search for you, like orphaned children. But you are not
where we had placed you. All we can find is the space in
which we had tried to contain you. 'You are looking for
me in places of death,' you tell us. 'But I am Life. The Life
you can never contain within a fixed idea.'

April 17th

Mary stayed outside near the tomb, weeping … Jesus said: 'Woman, why are you weeping? Who are you looking for?' Supposing him to be the gardener, she said: 'Sir, if you have taken him away, tell me where you have put him, and I will go and remove him.' Jesus said: 'Mary!' She knew him then and said to him in Hebrew, 'Rabbuni!' which means 'Master'.

(John 20:11–16)

Our teachers never told us this, Lord. Our books and courses never mentioned it. They taught us much *about* you. But we needed to hear you speak our name, before we could *know* you and, in that knowledge, know ourselves. And when you spoke our name, our response was easy and inevitable, and uttered in our own familiar language.

April 18th

'Why are you so agitated, and why are these doubts rising in your hearts? Look at my hands and feet; yes, it is I indeed. Touch me and see for yourselves; a ghost has no flesh and bones as you can see I have.'

(Luke 24:38–40)

A ghost might have been easier to cope with – more easily dismissed as a trick of the imagination. But instead you ask for our real, embodied, full-blooded response to your indestructible Reality, energising every particle of your creation.

April 19th

The disciples came on in the boat, towing the net and
the fish; they were only about a hundred yards from
land … Jesus said to them, 'Come and have
breakfast.' None of the disciples was bold enough
to ask, 'Who are you?' They knew quite well
it was the Lord.

(John 21:12)

There are still a hundred yards of water between me and
the impossible invitation. My mind tells my heart to look
before I leap, but my heart knows quite well who is
cooking my breakfast.

April 20th

*Mary of Magdala went to those who had been his
companions and who were mourning and in tears,
and told them.*

(Mark 16:10)

What we have seen, we must tell. For there is a world full
of mourning, aching for the touch of joy.

April 21st

You have made known the way of life to me,
you will fill me with gladness through your presence.

(Acts 2:28)

In the quiet of prayer, I notice those moments when my inner compass finds its still point in you. And that is the only trustworthy way I have found to read the map of my life's journey.

April 22nd

The disciples told their story of what had happened on the road and how they had recognised Jesus at the breaking of bread. They were still talking about all this when Jesus himself stood among them.

(Luke 24:35–36)

When we share our journeys in faith, trustfully, with each other, then we shall meet you, standing among us.

April 23rd

*When the officials brought the apostles in to face the
Sanhedrin, the high priest demanded an explanation.
'We gave you a formal warning,' he said, 'not to
preach in his name, and what have you done? You
have filled Jerusalem with your teaching.'*

(Acts 5:27–28)

Those who ran away and hid, those who denied you and
abandoned you and crouched in the upper room, afraid of
the authorities, have been filled with your risen presence,
and all Jerusalem cannot contain their courage and
their joy.

April 24th

Do not model yourselves on the behaviour of the world around you, but let your behaviour change, modelled by your new mind.

(Romans 12:2)

Our true shape is not the one imposed by the pressures around us, but the one that emerges from within us, where you dwell, as a flower emerges from a seed.

April 25th

Peter said [to the crippled beggar at the Temple gate]
'I have neither silver nor gold, but I will give you
what I have: in the name of Jesus Christ
the Nazarene, walk!'

(Acts 3:6)

The two friends rarely exchanged material gifts. There was
no need. Instead, they exchanged an unpossessive, uncon-
ditional love, through which each gave the other the
empowerment to become his true self, fully alive.

April 26th

Jesus called the people to him again and said, 'Listen to me, all of you, and understand. Nothing that goes into a man from outside can make him unclean; it is the things that come out of a man that make him unclean. For it is from within, from men's hearts, that evil intentions emerge.

(Mark 7:14–16, 21)

Help me to see, Lord, that it isn't the pressure of my circumstances that leads me away from you, but my way of reacting to them.

April 27th

Suddenly, while Saul was travelling to Damascus and just before he reached the city, there came a light from heaven all round him. He fell to the ground, and then he heard a voice saying, 'Saul, Saul, why are you persecuting me?'

(Acts 9:3–4)

Gemma's nerves had been stretched to breaking point, yet she knew there was no excuse for the way she had turned on her little son and made him the focus of all her frustration. It was nearly midnight when she went to bed, still seething with resentment. Something drew her into the nursery as she passed. The nightlight was still burning. Its glow fell like a ray from heaven across the child's tear-stained face. 'Gemma,' she seemed to hear her heart reproach her, 'why are you being so untrue to yourself?'

April 28th

*As they prayed, the house where they were assembled
rocked; they were all filled with the Holy Spirit and
began to proclaim the word of God boldly.*

(Acts 4:31)

We build up our defences, like a city in an earthquake
zone, but we know we are defenceless before the power of
your Spirit, and we trust that you will turn our helplessness into your strength.

April 29th

The wind blows where it pleases; you hear its sound,
but you cannot tell where it comes from or where
it is going. That is how it is with all who are
born of the Spirit.

(John 3:8)

We know, yet we know not, where we came from or where we are going. We only know that we are making the journey with you and, like the migrating geese, we must trust the guiding compass you give us by your steady, silent presence in our hearts.

April 30th

You sweep men away like a dream,
like grass which springs up in the morning.
In the morning it springs up and flowers:
by evening it withers and fades.

(Psalm 90:5–6)

As we watch the chicks of May take flight on their autumn
migrations – hatched yesterday and flown tomorrow – we
remember our own springing and fading, and we trust you
for the unseen harvest.

MAY

May 1st

At night there are tears, but joy comes with dawn ...
You have changed my mourning into dancing.

(Psalm 30:5, 11)

Today I can feel gratitude, even for the desert times and the pain and the heartache in the years that have passed. I can feel it sincerely, because the pain, as well as the joy, has brought me to this place where I stand today: a good place, a place of promise, which I am learning to trust.

May 2nd

*Jesus said to the Jews: 'How can you believe, since you
look to one another for approval and are not concerned
with the approval that comes from the one God?'*

(John 5:44)

When I was a child I lived under the constant need to
please others. As I grew up, I more often chose to please
myself. Only now do I begin to realise that all *you* ask of
me is that I should let myself become the person you
created me to be.

May 3rd

*'Can it be true that the authorities have made up
their minds that he is the Christ? Yet we all know
where he comes from, but when the Christ appears
no-one will know where he comes from.'*

(John 10:26, 27)

The last thing we expected was to find you sitting at the
next desk, standing behind us in the supermarket queue,
alongside us in the traffic jam. We had our eyes fixed to
the telescope and we failed to see the grass growing at
our feet.

May 4th

*While the Jews demand miracles and the Greeks look
for wisdom, here are we preaching a crucified Christ;
to the Jews an obstacle that they cannot get over, to
the pagans madness, but to those who have been
called, whether they are Jews or Greeks, a Christ who
is the power and the wisdom of God.*

(1 Corinthians 1:23–25)

Katy admired David's ability to engage the attention of
their friends in what he said and did, and she had great
respect for the understanding he revealed in their con-
versations and discussions, but it wasn't until she saw him,
weak and broken, in a hospital bed, that she knew how
much she *loved* him.

May 5th

The Jews gathered round him and said, 'How much longer are you going to keep us in suspense? If you are the Christ, tell us plainly.' Jesus replied: 'I have told you, but you do not believe.'

(John 10:24, 25)

A clear, unambiguous sign from God would change the world, like a universal change of government. But the Christ brings us something more permanent and more true: a change of heart.

May 6th

'Where two or three meet in my name, I shall be there with them.'

(Matthew 18:20)

Where your love flows through our human circles, they become mirrors of your Trinity, where each is bound to all and all to each, and every circle is centred on you.

May 7th

'I tell you most solemnly,
whoever welcomes the one I send welcomes me,
and whoever welcomes me welcomes the one
who sent me.'

(John 13:20)

The lone parent was new to the district. After the service was over, she left the church alone, with her boisterous toddler. The regular congregation wondered who she was, but nobody took the trouble to find out. Strange, that you should be unwelcome, in your own House.

May 8th

Thomas said, 'Lord, we do not know where you are going, so how can we know the way?' Jesus said: 'I am the Way, the Truth and the Life.'

(John 14:6)

I don't need to know the way; I am on a journey where everyone I meet is my destination, for in everyone I meet, I meet You.

May 9th

*Philip said: 'Lord, let us see the Father and then we
shall be satisfied.' 'Have I been with you all this time,
Philip,' said Jesus to him, 'and you still do not know
me? To have seen me is to have seen the Father.'*

(John 14:8, 9)

I hold a fallen berry in my hand. It contains the complete
genetic code of the tree from which it sprang. The berry
will grow into the tree and the tree will yield the
berry. When I touch the berry, I touch the meaning of
the tree.

May 10th

Jesus took with him Peter and John and James and went up the mountain to pray. As he prayed, the aspect of his face was changed and his clothing became brilliant as lightning.

(Luke 9:28)

I watched as two people walked across the station forecourt. One was a tall, strong young man. He had his arm round the shoulder of his companion, who was stooped, frail in mind and body, chattering meaninglessly, and ageless in his suffering. The strong man walked slowly, matching his pace to that of his companion. There was no sign of impatience in his face, or reluctance in his sheltering arm. He was listening to him intently, as if to a guru. They reached the escalator, and carefully descended, out of my sight. I shook myself, inwardly, and I knew that Christ had crossed my path, and that I had seen his radiance in a city station.

May 11th

In you all find their home.

(Psalm 87:7)

There were some unlikely bedfellows in the Animal Rescue Centre. In the wild they would have been implacable enemies, or predators, one upon the other. But in their pain and their helplessness they lay side by side, drawn together by the loving care that ministered to them.

May 12th

The Lord is my strength and my shield;
In him my heart trusts.

(Psalm 28:7)

How strong is my trust in you, Lord? Weaker than the power of my greatest fear! But you are asking me to trust that your power is greater than the combined force of all my fears, all the world's fears. And such trust is possible, because you have pinned it on the cross for all to see and share.

May 13th

When he was near the gate of the town of Nain,
it happened that a dead man was being carried out
for burial, the only son of his mother, and she was
a widow. When the Lord saw her he felt sorry
for her. 'Do not cry,' he said. Then he went up and
put his hand on the bier and the bearers stood still
and he said 'Young man, I tell you to get up.'
And the dead man sat up and began to talk,
and Jesus gave him to his mother.

(Luke 7:11–16)

The miracle of healing begins with compassion and leads
to the giving back of life. Give us compassion for each
other, Lord, that we too may restore each other to the
fullness of life.

May 14th

I have made you a light for the nations,
so that my salvation may reach the ends of the earth.

(Acts 13:47)

When I blow out my prayer candle, the wisps of smoke float off into every remote corner of the house. Prayer begins for real when the light goes *out* – out into the dark places.

May 15th

*Jesus made his way through towns and villages
preaching, and proclaiming the Good News of the
kingdom of God. With him went the Twelve, as well
as certain women who had been cured of evil spirits
and ailments.*

(Luke 8:1–2)

Five minutes in the presence of someone who has been
cured of what is ailing me is more precious to me than an
hour of expert consultancy.

May 16th

'I am the vine, you are the branches.
Whoever remains in me, with me in him,
bears fruit in plenty,
for cut off from me you can do nothing.

(John 15:5)

The wood is carpeted with bluebells. Every May they flood my heart with their joyful exuberance of blue. Year in, year out, their fragile bulbs break out again into the fullness of their living. Yet how dispiriting is the sight of a jug of bluebells, plucked at dawn and, by midday, drooping sadly down to premature death.

May 17th

*A sower went out to sow his seed. As he sowed some
fell on the edge of the path and was trampled on; and
the birds of the air ate it up. Some seed fell on rock,
and when it came up it withered away, having no
moisture. Some seed fell amongst thorns and the
thorns grew with it and choked it. And some seed
fell into rich soil and grew and produced its crop
a hundredfold.*

(Luke 8:5–8)

Sometimes the seed of your truth falls onto my soil
through the wisdom of a friend or neighbour. But I feel
threatened by it and trample it to death. Or I receive it
with a stony silence, and deprive it of life-giving encour-
agement. Or I crowd it out with my own concerns and
ideas and choke it. Please give me the grace to give your
seed the space for growth and fruitfulness.

May 18th

'You do not choose me, no, I chose you;
and I commissioned you to go out and to bear fruit,
fruit that will last.'

(John 15:16)

The mother watched patiently as her child made his options. Choosing subjects, choosing a job, choosing friends. He was sure that he was in control, yet she had made the choice that made all other choices possible: the choice to give him life.

May 19th

*'If they persecuted me, they will persecute you too;
if they kept my word, they will keep your word
as well.'*

(John 15:20)

When we run up against the rock face, let us remember
that you ran up against it too. You were broken against it,
so that the seeds of eternal life might be released. Seeds
that settle and take root in the rocks of persecution,
breaking down the hardness, bringing life.

May 20th

May you be blessed by the Lord,
the maker of heaven and earth.
The heavens belong to the Lord,
but the earth he has given to men.

(Psalm 115:15–16)

We feel pangs of hurt and sadness if we realise that a gift we have given in love is neglected, or used carelessly, or even wilfully damaged. How do *you* feel, Lord, when you see how we treat your gift to us of this earth, our home?

May 21st

Now we are seeing a dim reflection in a mirror; but then we shall be seeing face to face. The knowledge that I have now is imperfect; but then I shall know as fully as I am known.

(1 Corinthians 13:12)

When I stop looking at my own mirror image, and turn instead to look into *your* face, then, at last, in your clear, love-filled gaze, I shall see your promise of who I really am.

May 22nd

*'Simon,' Jesus said, 'you see this woman? ... I tell
you that her sins, her many sins, must have been
forgiven her, or she would not have shown such great
love. It is the man who is forgiven little who shows
little love.'*

(Luke 7:47)

If we are tempted to feel that we love you more than
others do, help us to remember, Lord, that the measure of
our love for you is the measure of the forgiveness you have
poured out upon us, and the measure of that forgiveness is
the measure of our need of it.

May 23rd

Hide me in the shadow of your wings.

(Psalm 17:8)

When I feel weak, I run to you for shelter, like a chick to the mother hen. When I feel strong, let me not forget that it is your eagles' wings that are carrying me above the storm.

May 24th

*Jesus said to his disciples: 'Now I am going to the one
who sent me. Not one of you has asked, "Where are
you going?" Yet you are sad at heart because I have
told you this. Still I must tell you the truth: it is for
your own good that I am going, because unless I go
the Advocate will not come to you.'*

(John 16:5–7)

In the dark times of our prayer you seem to have with-
drawn far beyond the reach of our minds and senses. Yet
the darkness reveals the stars, and the cloud that receives
you holds the promise of an unimaginable new dawning
of power and love.

May 25th

*In fact he is not far from any of us, since it is in him
that we live, and move, and exist.*

(Acts 17:27–28)

The tiny oak leaves are just beginning to unfurl, and are
waking up to springtime. If I could tell them about the
vast network of branch and trunk and root that holds them
in being, they would never believe me. An obvious reality
for me – an impossible leap of imagination for them. How
far am I, then, from understanding the sources of your love
that hold me in being?

May 26th

'And know that I am with you always;
yes, to the end of time.'

(Matthew 28:20)

With us always ... even then, when we are walking away from you ... especially then, when we are sure we can manage without you ... and precisely then, when we feel you have given up on us ... With us always, and closer to us than we are to ourselves.

May 27th

'A woman in childbirth suffers, because her time has come; but when she has given birth to the child she forgets the suffering in her joy that a child has been born into the world.'

(John 16:21)

The final stage of labour seemed to last for hours. I started to think: 'This child isn't ever going to be born,' but my common sense knew better. When I start to wonder whether your kingdom will ever come, I remember the moment when the midwife placed my daughter in my arms. And I believe.

May 28th

'Ask and you will receive, and so your joy
will be complete.'

(John 16:24)

I asked for food and you taught me how to fish. I asked for
security and you gave me the freedom to live without fear.
I asked for happiness, and you gave me joy. I come to you
with the leaves and petals of my desires, but you satisfy
their roots.

May 29th

*'They will expel you from the synagogues, and
indeed the hour is coming when anyone who kills you
will think he is doing a holy duty for God. They will
do these things because they have never known
either the Father or myself.'*

(John 16:2–3)

The gulf between Barbara and her son widened daily as
their quarrel over his girlfriend deepened. Barbara refused
to have the girl in the house or to hear anything good
about her. 'If you *knew* her you wouldn't react like this,' he
protested. But Barbara didn't *want* to know.

May 30th

*Late that night Paul and Silas were praying and
singing God's praises, while the other prisoners
listened. Suddenly there was an earthquake that
shook the prison to its foundations. All the doors flew
open and the chains fell from all the prisoners.*

(Acts 16:25–26)

The earth-shaking force of our lives' worst experiences
can bring about the radical re-making that prepares us for
our lives' most powerful growth and opens up the doors of
our hearts to your redeeming liberation.

May 31st

*So now the Lord of hosts says this: Reflect carefully
how things have gone for you. You have sown much
and harvested little; you eat but never have enough,
drink but never have your fill, put on clothes but do
not feel warm. The wage earner gets his wages only to
put them in a purse riddled with holes.*

(Haggai 1:5–8)

When I bank my wages, Lord, help me to remember
that I am dealing with a dangerously addictive substance
that, without your grace, will leave me for ever longing
for more.

JUNE

June 1st

'You are sad now, but I shall see you again,
and your hearts will be full of joy,
and that joy no one shall take from you.'

(John 16:22)

We may gather happiness painlessly, like blackberries at the roadside, easily reached. But joy is a more elusive fruit, and often lies beyond a barrier of thorns, and on the other side of sorrow.

June 2nd

You poured down, O God, a generous rain:
when your people were starved you gave them
new life.

(Psalm 68:9)

Not just watering-cans, to keep us going through the hard
times, but generous, soaking, saturating grace that brings
life out of our most deeply-buried roots.

June 3rd

'Father, may they be one in us, as you are in me and I am in you.'

(John 17:21)

Paul is blind. Tomorrow he leaves for a holiday in Italy with his sighted brother-in-law, Jim. Jim speaks no Italian, but Paul is fluent in the language. They joke, as they pack: 'I'll be his tongue, and he'll be my eyes,' says Paul. Lord, may our unity in you lead us to a fullness that is infinitely greater than the sum of our separate selves.

June 4th

'I tell you most solemnly, when you were young, you put on your own belt and walked where you liked, but when you grow old you will stretch out your hands, and somebody else will put a belt round you and take you where you would rather not go.'

(John 21:18)

When I began my journey of faith, I felt strong and sure and I thought I knew where I was going. But the further I travelled, the more I became aware of my ever-growing helplessness and inadequacy, and my absolute need of you.

June 5th

There were many other things that Jesus did;
if all were written down, the world itself,
I suppose, would not hold all the books that would
have to be written.

(John 21:25)

And if each of us were to tell of all the ways that God has
touched our lives and our hearts, the world itself could not
contain all our stories.

June 6th

*'I have told you all this so that you may find peace
in me. In the world you will have trouble, but be
brave; I have conquered the world.'*

(John 16:33)

Armchair believing may provide a comfortable sanctuary
amid life's storms, but our faith becomes authentic when
it is sharpened on the cutting edge of challenge and of
struggle and of opposition.

June 7th

One day when Jesus was praying alone in the
presence of his disciples he put this question to them,
'Who do the crowds say I am?' And they answered,
'John the Baptist; others Elijah; and others say one of
the ancient prophets come back to life.' 'But you,' he
said, 'who do you say I am?'

(Luke 9:18–20)

The five-year-olds were coming out of school at the end
of their first day. 'Which one's your Mum?' David asked
Jim. 'I know her, she's the lady at the checkout in the
supermarket,' broke in Simon. 'No, she's our Sunday
School teacher,' David corrected him. Only Jim knew the
full truth. He ran up to her and gave her a big hug, because
only he knew who she *really* was.

June 8th

*'I am not asking you to remove them from the world,
but to protect them from the evil one.'*

(John 17:15)

When the storms blow against me, my instinctive prayer is
to ask you to transplant me to a safer, more welcoming
place. You answer my prayer by leaving me where I am, in
the eye of the storm, but by strengthening and deepening
the roots of my life, down to their true centre in you.

June 9th

*Then he said to him a third time: 'Simon, son of
John, do you love me?' Peter said, 'Lord, you know
everything; you know I love you.' Jesus said to him:
'Feed my sheep.'*

(John 21:17)

The test of our loving is always in the warmth of our
giving.

June 10th

*Let all who are thirsty come; all who want it may
have the water of life, and have it free.*

(Revelation 22:17)

Water, source of life, without droughts or standpipes, without bills and without shareholders. The only qualification for receiving it is to *want* it.

June 11th

*At a time when everyone was full of admiration for
all he did, Jesus said to his disciples, 'For your part,
you must have these words constantly in mind: the
Son of Man is going to be handed over into the
power of men.'*

(Luke 9:43–44)

The crowds follow you eagerly, Lord, all wanting to be
with you, to be part of who you are. We see ourselves
among them. But the road leads to Jerusalem, to betrayal,
to suffering and to death. Can we hear your warning
words? And will we follow you anyway?

June 12th

Do not say to your neighbour: 'Go away!
Come another time. I will give it you tomorrow,'
if you can do it now.

(Proverbs 3:28)

Mary had to pass old Hannah's door every day when she came home from work. During the cold snap she even wondered whether Hannah was keeping warm enough, and whether perhaps she should go round and check. Then one evening she saw the police car and ambulance parked outside. The finality of death had frozen her good intentions into inescapable reproach.

June 13th

As long as earth lasts,
sowing and reaping,
cold and heat,
summer and winter,
day and night
shall cease no more.

(Genesis 8:22)

Today may have felt like a disaster. This year may have seemed like a failure. But our days and years are held in a vast continuum of life, and you have promised that this life is leading all your children home to your eternal love.

June 14th

God said, 'Here is the sign of the Covenant I make
between myself and you and every living creature
with you for all generations: I set my bow in
the clouds and it shall be a sign of the
Covenant between me and the earth.'

(Genesis 9:12–13)

Give us the grace to see beyond the stinging of our tears
to the radiance of your promise, eternally shining through
the clouds.

June 15th

'Come,' they said, 'let us build ourselves a town and a tower with its top reaching heaven. Let us make a name for ourselves … It was named Babel … It was from there that the Lord scattered them over the whole face of the earth.'

(Genesis 11:4, 9)

Jim had plenty of time to look back over his life, as he lived out his declining years in the nursing home, unvisited and unloved. In his hey-day he had built a business empire out of nothing. He had made a name for himself. He had reached for the stars. But in the process he had lost all connection with his family and friends. They had scattered far and wide beyond his reach, and now he was a nameless old man, laid low by loneliness and regret.

June 16th

*Only faith can guarantee the blessings that we hope
for, or prove the existence of the realities that at
present remain unseen.*

(Hebrews 11:1)

Carol was so proud of her son who had persevered
through chronic illness and disability, to become the wise
and cheerful adult he had grown into. 'I could only do it,
Mum,' he said, 'because you believed in me.'

June 17th

The father of the boy (in convulsions) cried out: 'I do
have faith. Help the little faith I have.'

(Mark 9:25)

We may have beliefs enough to fill a catechism, but do we
trust you, Lord? We may believe in everything we read on
the seed packet, but will we plant the seed? And will we
tend its growing?

June 18th

'Anyone who welcomes one of these little children in my name, welcomes me, and anyone who welcomes me welcomes not me but the one who sent me.'

(Mark 9:37)

The one who can see the bird inside the egg and the oak inside the acorn, can see the Lord of all creation in a little child.

June 19th

'Anyone who is not against us is for us.'

(Mark 9:40)

I would rather assume that everyone is friendly, and be fooled a few times, but keep my heart open to everyone around me, than hold my image and my wallet safe, but die with a closed-up heart.

June 20th

'Jerusalem, Jerusalem ... How often I have longed to gather your children, as a hen gathers her brood under her wings, and you refused.'

(Luke 13:34)

The mallard mother quickly tried to gather her six ducklings together in safety, when she sensed the vibrations of the approaching motor boat. One of them refused. And then there were five.

*'As for those who do not welcome you, when you
leave their town shake the dust from your feet
as a sign to them.'*

(Luke 9:5)

The dust of old hurts and resentments accumulates and clings to my feet like a solid layer of mud, until it finally prevents me from moving on at all. To shake it off is to set myself free, as well as those who caused the hurting.

June 22nd

He then said, 'Go, eat the fat, drink the sweet wine,
and send a portion to the man who has nothing
prepared ready. For this day is sacred to our Lord.
Do not be sad: the joy of the Lord is
your stronghold.'

(Nehemiah 8:10–11)

You ask only this of those who come to your table: that we
enjoy your feast, and that we *share* it.

June 23rd

It was then that, filled with joy by the Holy Spirit,
he said, 'I bless you, Father, Lord of heaven and of
earth, for hiding these things from the learned
and the clever and revealing them to
mere children.'

(Luke 10:21)

As we build the mountains of knowledge in our children's
minds, help us to tread carefully, lest we bury the treasure
of wisdom that you have planted in their hearts.

June 24th

You never know what will happen tomorrow:
you are no more than a mist that is here for a little
while and then disappears.

(James 4:14)

A mist can obscure the beauty of life, from ourselves and
from others. Or it can soak into the earth and give life to
new growth. Which shall our lives become: an obscuring
cloud, or a refreshing dewfall?

June 25th

'Naked I came from my mother's womb,
naked I shall return.
The Lord gave, the Lord has taken back.
Blessed be the name of the Lord!'

(Job 1:21)

When gain and loss become as simple as breathing in and breathing out, then we shall begin to see how close you have been to us when we thought we were most grievously alone.

June 26th

If you mean 'Yes', you must say 'Yes';
if you mean 'No', say 'No.'

(James 5:12)

The hallmark of truth is its simplicity. Complications and convolutions are the symptoms of concealment. Simplicity is of God. The complications are our own.

June 27th

*My brothers, if one of you strays away from the truth
and another brings him back to it, he may be sure that
anyone who can bring back a sinner from the wrong
way that he has taken will be saving a soul from
death and covering up a great number of sins.*

(James 5:20)

One return to the way of truth is worth a hundred
reproaches for deviating from it.

June 28th

*Jesus looked steadily at him and loved him, and he
said: 'There is one thing you lack. Go and sell
everything you own and give the money to the poor,
and you will have treasure in heaven; then come,
follow me.'*

(Mark 10:21–22)

Arnold lay dying, surrounded by all his memories – everything that he had valued and loved in life. Day by day he
loosened himself from everything, saying goodbye with
gratitude, not with regret. And when he was free of everything that held him, he was light enough to follow you
into eternal life.

June 29th

*As Jesus and his disciples travelled along
they met a man on the road who said to him:
'I will follow you wherever you go.'*

(Luke 9:57)

To follow wherever *you* go is to court humiliation and
contempt, disgrace and destruction. Our following of you
may take us to the depths of hell, but it will never lead
where you have not walked yourself.

June 30th

O Lord, you search me and you know me,
you know my resting and my rising,
you discern my purpose from afar.
You mark when I walk or lie down,
all my ways lie open to you.

(Psalm 139:1–3)

Once it filled me with apprehension, that nothing I could do or say or think could be concealed from you. Now it fills me with hope and trust, knowing that whatever paths lie before me, everything has the potential to lead me to you.

JULY

July 1st

Job died, an old man and full of days.

(Job 42:16)

To die an old man is one thing; but to have lived a life in which every day was really *lived*, that is quite another.

July 2nd

The word of the Lord was addressed to Jonah son of Amittai: 'Up!' he said 'Go to Nineveh, the great city, and inform them that their wickedness has become known to me.' Jonah decided to run away from the Lord, and go to Tarshish. He went down to Joppa and found a ship bound for Tarshish; he paid his fare and went aboard, to go with them to Tarshish, to get away from the Lord. But the Lord unleashed a violent wind on the sea, and there was such a great storm at sea that the ship threatened to break up.

(Jonah 1:1–5)

I *know* when I am trying to avoid your stirrings in my life, and run away from your guiding. I know it because the turmoil inside me rises to storm force and my life starts to come apart at the seams.

July 3rd

Martha, who was distracted with all the serving said,
'Lord, do you not care that my sister is leaving me
to do the serving all by myself? Please tell her to
help me.' But the Lord answered: 'Martha, Martha,'
he said, 'you worry and fret about so many things,
and yet few are needed, indeed only one. It is
Mary who has chosen the better part; it is not
to be taken from her.'

(Luke 10:40–42)

By the evening Christine felt exhausted and fragmented.
She felt as if she had been all things to all people: wife,
mother, colleague, friend, secretary, teacher and nurse. She
lay awake in bed, too tired to sleep, and watched the sky.
One single star shone out above her. It steadied her heart,
until she could hear your voice inside her: 'For me, you are
one; you are whole; you are Christine.'

July 4th

*Once Jesus was in a certain place praying, and
when he had finished, one of his disciples said,
'Lord, teach us to pray.'*

(Luke 11:1)

We learn to pray by being in the presence of the One who
is always in his Father's presence.

July 5th

*'What man among you with a hundred sheep, losing
one would not leave the ninety-nine in the wilderness
and go after the missing one till he found it? ... I tell
you, there will be more rejoicing in heaven over one
repentant sinner than over ninety-nine virtuous men
who have no need of repentance.'*

(Luke 15:4, 7)

Ted had all he needed, but still he spent most of his time
in his old rocking-chair. It was polished with age and wear
now, but he would never forget that, years ago, he had
found it, mildewed, splintered and abandoned, at the tip. It
had taken him years to restore it and now it meant everything to him. He had invested his heart in it, and made it
live again.

July 6th

The nations have fallen in the pit which they made,
their feet caught in the snare they laid.

(Psalm 9:15)

There is a causal connection between the greed and pride
of empire and the barbarity and squalor of war. There is a
causal connection between our every selfish gesture and
the deep discontent that reigns in and around us.

July 7th

*The children of this world are more astute in dealing
with their own kind than are the children of light.*

(Luke 16:8)

Gary regularly submitted fraudulent benefit claims while
he went on moonlighting.

Andrew did it once, out of desperation.

Gary knew how to cover his tracks. It was Andrew who
was caught.

Gary never gave it a second thought. Andrew was shattered by remorse.

July 8th

When that day comes,
the mountains will run with new wine
and the hills flow with milk,
and all the river beds of Judah
will run with water.

(Joel 4:18)

When God breaks out inside us, something overflows: nourishing, intoxicating, unceasingly replenished. Then God is in flood, and there will be an abundant harvest. And God is always in flood, unless we block the flow.

July 9th

The tenants of the master's vineyard said to each other: 'This is the heir. Come on, let us kill him and the inheritance will be ours.' So they seized him and killed him and threw him out of the vineyard.

(Mark 12:7–8)

What we take by force, we may hold for a season. What you give through grace is our inheritance for all eternity.

July 10th

They handed him a denarius and he said:
'Whose head is this? Whose name?' 'Caesar's,'
they told him. Jesus said to them, 'Give back to
Caesar what belongs to Caesar – and to God what
belongs to God.'

(Mark 12:15–17)

How shall I draw my life's energy? In the currency of
Caesar, with its punitive interest rates? Or in the currency
of God, that is given unearned?

July 11th

'I will give you a new commandment: love one another; you must love one another just as I have loved you. It is by your love for one another that everyone will recognise you as my disciples.'

(John 13:34–35)

Love is not an optional extra, to warm and soften our ways of living and relating; rather our ways of living and relating are the ways in which the Love that holds us in being finds its embodied expression.

July 12th

*One of the scribes came up to Jesus and put a
question to him: 'Which is the first of all the
commandments?' Jesus replied: 'This is the first.
Listen, Israel, the Lord your God is the one Lord,
and you must love the Lord your God with all your
heart, with all your soul, with all your mind and with
all your strength. The second is this: you must love
your neighbour as yourself. There is no commandment
greater than these.'*

(Mark 12:28–31)

All of me: not just the Sunday slot. All of me: not just my
conscious thoughts. All of me: not just the span of years I
call my life on earth. All of me: just space enough to hold
a seed of God.

July 13th

It is the Lord who keeps faith for ever,
who is just to those who are oppressed.
It is he who gives bread to the hungry,
the Lord, who sets prisoners free.

(Psalm 146:6–7)

When we look into the eyes of one who is caring for the oppressed, the hungry, the prisoners, we are looking into the heart of God, whether the one who is caring is aware of God or not.

July 14th

*He sat down opposite the treasury and watched the
people putting money into the treasury, and many of
the rich put in a great deal. A poor widow came and
put in two small coins, the equivalent of a penny.
Then he called his disciples and said to them: 'I tell
you solemnly, this poor widow has put in more than
all who have contributed to the treasury; for they have
all put in money they had over, but she from the little
she had has put in everything she possessed, all she
had to live on.'*

(Mark 12:41–44)

My eyes were blinded by the tears that the ugly incident
had caused. The richest gifts, the most lavish promises,
would have left me unconsoled. Then my two-year-old
came up to me, looked at me with mute, sad eyes, and
placed her teddy in my lap. It was everything she had: it
was everything I needed.

July 15th

> '*A Samaritan traveller who came upon him was*
> *moved with compassion when he saw him. He went*
> *up and bandaged his wounds, pouring oil and wine on*
> *them. He then lifted him onto his own mount, carried*
> *him to the inn and looked after him.*'

(Luke 10:33–34)

A crowd of bystanders gathered round the scene of the accident. They watched the paramedics carrying the old lady to the ambulance, and they were relieved that none of their own family had been involved. In the emergency ward the nurses did all they could to ease her pain and bind her wounds, but there was neither the time nor the funding for any more. It was when she was sent home that the unemployed immigrant family from next-door came round. They turned their compassion into an unobtrusive, undemanding, day-by-day caring for their wounded neighbour.

July 16th

Show forth your work to your servants;
let your glory shine on their children.

(Psalm 90:16–17)

The brilliance of the full moon held me rooted to the spot in awe and wonder. Yet it was only a lump of rock spinning through space, and its glory came entirely from the light of the unseen sun, shining upon it in the darkness of my night. It shed upon me its promise that we too, your lumps of clay, might reflect the light of *your* unseen presence into the darkness we find around us.

July 17th

He is God, not of the dead, but of the living.

(Mark 12:27)

When I dwell on the follies and the failures of the past, I find nothing but an empty tomb. But when I hear you call my name in the garden of my grief, I know that you are touching that which is alive in me, and calling it into resurrection.

July 18th

Two men went up to the Temple to pray, one a Pharisee, the other a tax collector. The Pharisee stood there and said this prayer to himself: 'I thank you, God, that I am not grasping, unjust, adulterous, like the rest of mankind, and particularly that I am not like this tax collector here. I fast twice a week; I pay tithes on all I get.' The tax collector stood some distance away, not daring even to raise his eyes to heaven; but he beat his breast and said, 'God, be merciful to me, a sinner.'

(Luke 18:9–13)

When I think of the things that I do best in life, and feel the satisfaction of doing them better than my friends or colleagues, then I meet my inner Pharisee, who points her finger at me with the words 'And *you* thought you were a tax collector!'

July 19th

You are, all of you, sons of God through faith in Christ Jesus. All baptised in Christ, you have clothed yourselves in Christ.

(Galatians 3:26–27)

When I am dressed for the ball, I don't go wading through the mud. Lord, may the ways of my heart and the pattern of my living become consistent with the words in which I clothe my faith.

July 20th

As for me, my life is already being poured away as a libation, and the time has come for me to be gone.

(2 Timothy 4:6)

The power of your Spirit in our hearts is only released when we take the risk of our own emptying and allow you to pour us out for others.

July 21st

'Anyone who tries to preserve his life will lose it;
and anyone who loses it will keep it safe.'

(Luke 17:33)

Lydia refused to get into the lifeboat without her bag of valuables. Her fellow passengers, shivering and bereft, were rowed to safety. Lydia still lies, with her treasure, in the wreckage on the ocean bed.

July 22nd

*Peter went up to Jesus and said, 'Lord, how often
must I forgive my brother if he wrongs me? As often
as seven times?' Jesus answered, 'Not seven, I tell you,
but seventy-seven times.*

(Matthew 18:21–22)

Just when I thought I had finally forgiven him, a chance
remark awakened all my old resentments. How deep must
my forgiveness go, Lord? From the quiver on my lips
through the tears in my eyes, right down to the gash in
my heart!

July 23rd

You say that you have faith and I have good deeds;
I will prove to you that I have faith by showing you
my good deeds — now you prove to me that you have
faith without any good deeds to show.

(James 2:18)

When I pick a ripe, healthy apple, I know that the apple
tree has sound, deep roots, but if there are no apples on the
tree, how can I know that the tree is alive at all?

July 24th

*We are only the earthenware jars that hold this
treasure, to make it clear that such an overwhelming
power comes from God and not from us.*

(2 Corinthians 4:7)

... and even when we are shattered, the worst that can
happen is that God's love and grace and power spill over
into the waiting world.

July 25th

*The Lord spoke to Moses, 'Go down now, because your
people whom you brought out of Egypt have apostasised
… They have made themselves a calf of molten metal
and have worshipped it … Leave me now, my wrath
shall blaze out against them and devour them; of you,
however, I will make a great nation …' But Moses
pleaded with the Lord his God. 'Lord,' he said, 'why
should your wrath blaze out against this people of
yours …?' So the Lord relented.*

(Exodus 32:7–11, 14)

Janet and Jean were both terrified by their mother's fury,
even though the damage was entirely Jean's fault. Eventually
Janet went to their mother and begged her not to punish
Jean. Her mother looked at them both and her eyes
softened. In that moment she saw just how much Janet
loved her sister. It was a love strong enough to heal the
relationship between the three of them.

July 26th

*My thoughts are not your thoughts, my ways are not
your ways – it is the Lord who speaks. Yes, the
heavens are as high above the earth as my
thoughts above your thoughts.*

(Isaiah 55:8–9)

My image of you is as far removed from your reality as a
pinpoint of starlight in the night sky is removed from the
fiery sun that is its source. Help me to see that it is only
my distance from you that makes the difference.

July 27th

You have put into my heart a greater joy than they
have from abundance of corn and new wine.

(Psalm 4:7)

We rejoice briefly in the harvest suppers of our lives,
but *you* give a joy that will sustain us all through
our wintering.

July 28th

Peacemakers, when they work for peace, sow the seeds which will bear fruit in holiness.

(James 3:18)

Making peace, whether in the everyday of family life or in the arena of international affairs, can feel like ploughing through a muddy, unyielding field, yet without that heartbreaking, backbreaking toil, you will have nowhere to scatter the seeds of love.

July 29th

And thus you provide for the earth;
you drench its furrows,
you level it, soften it with showers,
you bless its growth.

(Psalm 65:10)

Sometimes our lives fill up with sorrow and the sharp blades of pain drive furrows through our hearts. Saturate us, then, with your grace, so that we might know that, in just such times, you are blessing and nourishing our growth.

July 30th

*'If your right hand should cause you to sin, cut it
off and throw it away, for it will do you less harm to
lose one part of you than to have your whole body
go to hell.'*

(Matthew 5:30)

When I look around the inner rooms of my heart I find
gifts from you, which I have allowed to become the centre of my life. Help me to give them back to you, Lord,
and to build my life on the Giver and not the gifts.

July 31st

John said to Jesus, 'Master, we saw a man who is not
one of us casting out devils in your name; and because
he was not one of us we tried to stop him.' But Jesus
said, 'You must not stop him: no-one who works a
miracle in my name is likely to speak evil of me.
Anyone who is not against us is for us.'

(Mark 9:38–40)

The good news of your love is all-inclusive, Lord. Any
exclusions are of our own making, not of yours.

AUGUST

August 1st

Jesus said: 'And if anyone orders you to go one mile,
go two miles with him.'

(Matthew 5:42)

I simmer inwardly as I force myself to do the chores that
life imposes on me. For the first mile I feel like a slave. Yet
when the obligation is lifted I can do exactly the same
tasks again, in a free spirit, and discover joy in doing them.
I walk the second mile like a prince.

August 2nd

'But I say this to you: love your enemies and pray for those who persecute you; in this way you will be sons of your Father in heaven, for he causes his sun to rise on bad men as well as good, and his rain to fall on honest and dishonest men alike.'

(Matthew 5:44–46)

I need all my energy for living towards your fullness. The energy I expend in anger and resentment is diverted and lost. The energy I use for loving and praying is multiplied. It helps to neutralise my enemy's destructive feelings and it protects me from my own.

August 3rd

*'When you pray, go to your private room and, when
you have shut your door, pray to your Father who is
in that secret place, and your Father who sees all that
is done in secret will reward you.'*

(Matthew 6:6)

The Israelites carried Yahweh with them on their journeying, in the tabernacle-tent. To pray is to discover our
own tabernacle-tents in the deep silence of our hearts and
to enter its secret, sacred space to meet with the Lord of
the journey.

August 4th

*Jesus said to his disciples: 'In your prayers do not
babble as the pagans do, for they think that by using
many words they will make themselves heard.
Do not be like them; your Father knows what you
need before you ask him.'*

(Matthew 6:7–8)

In the excitement of first meeting, the friends hardly
stopped talking. But as their friendship deepened, they
discovered that their most profound feelings could only be
communicated in a receptive silence.

August 5th

Sing a new song to the Lord,
for he has worked wonders.

(Psalm 98:1)

The world has turned through millions of years since life began, yet still the song of every life is uniquely new and fresh and brings joy to you, our creator.

August 6th

'That is why I am telling you not to worry about your life and what you are to eat, nor about your body and how you are to clothe it. Surely life means more than food, and the body more than clothing! ...
Set your hearts on his kingdom first, and on his righteousness, and all these other things will be given you as well. So do not worry about tomorrow: tomorrow will take care of itself.'

(Matthew 6:25, 33–34)

The day had been so hectic. She had spent hours in the kitchen devising something to tempt the baby's appetite. Then she had rushed round the shops, searching for toys for his birthday. She sighed, as she leaned over his cot that night and stroked his sleeping head, with its soft, downy hair. The day was over, and she had come close to missing it completely. It would never return. He was a day older, and she was a day wiser.

August 7th

*'Give to anyone who asks, and if anyone wants to
borrow, do not turn away.'*

(Matthew 5:42)

Peter was getting tired of opening the door to beggars and
vagrants. Enough was enough. Then Charlie knocked.
And Peter looked into his eyes. And Peter gave again. And
a tear of gratitude trickled across Charlie's cheek. There
will never be enough of giving, until all is spent.

August 8th

Have mercy on me, God, in your kindness.
In your compassion blot out my offence.
O wash me more and more from my guilt
and cleanse me from my sin.

(Psalm 51:1–2)

The pick-axe of reproach may hack at our stony hearts, but only the ceaseless, gentle, cleansing flow of grace will soften them into flesh.

August 9th

*'When you give alms, your left hand must not know
what your right hand is doing; your almsgiving must
be secret, and your Father who sees all that is done in
secret will reward you.'*

(Matthew 6:3–4)

Everyone in the neighbourhood knew of Eileen's legendary generosity. Everyone, that is, except Eileen herself, who never gave it a thought, as she lived out her life in unself-conscious attentiveness to the needs of those around her.

August 10th

The Pharisee was surprised that Jesus had not first washed before the meal. But the Lord said to him 'Oh, you Pharisees! You clean the outside of cup and plate, while inside yourselves you are filled with extortion and wickedness.'

(Luke 11:38–39)

Aunt Agatha kept an immaculate household, and insisted on orderly behaviour in her home. She cringed as her small nephew came bursting in from the garden with muddy feet and sticky hands. But her protests were stifled by his exuberant hug, and the stiffness in her heart was softened by the warmth of his dirty face.

August 11th

'Where your treasure is, there will your heart be also.'

(Matthew 6:21)

It began harmlessly for Jim. First a few overtime hours, for an extra holiday, then a few more, for a bigger house, and finally a compulsive, workaholic lifestyle leaving him heart-strangled on the beaches of his ebbing life.

August 12th

I will punish their offences with the rod,
I will scourge them on account of their guilt.
But I will never take back my love:
my truth will never fail.

(Psalm 89:32–33)

It had been a terrible day, and Susan's temper was in shreds. A fractious toddler, a disobedient child and a moody teenager had all taken their toll on their mother's nerves. Finally, in the silence of the night, she slipped into their rooms one last time. As she kissed them softly in their sleep, her heart tugged itself back into place, and she knew, again, just how much she loved them.

August 13th

Zacchaeus was anxious to see what kind of man Jesus was, but he was too short and could not see him for the crowd; so he ran ahead and climbed a sycamore tree to catch a glimpse of Jesus who was to pass that way. When Jesus reached the spot he looked up and spoke to him: 'Zacchaeus, come down. Hurry, because I must stay at your house today.'

(Luke 19:3–6)

My only thought was to get a little closer to you, to get a better view. Yet that unspoken desire was all you needed to bring you to the very spot where I was so precariously perched. 'I'm looking for companions,' you said, 'not onlookers. Are you coming down?'

August 14th

Abram was a very rich man, with livestock, silver and gold. Lot, who was travelling with Abram, had flocks and cattle of his own and tents too. The land was not sufficient to accommodate them both at once, for they had too many possessions to be able to live together.

(Genesis 13:2)

Archaeologists tell us that the first general evidence of murder is linked to the time when people ceased to be nomadic and started to settle in one place, accumulate possessions and envy each others' treasures. From then on, they had too many possessions to be able to live together.

August 15th

In God alone is my soul at rest;
my help comes from him.
He alone is my rock, my stronghold,
my fortress: I stand firm.

(Psalm 62:1–2)

Beneath the most turbulent waves of my life lie the still and silent ocean depths of prayer. And beneath the depths, holding them in the palms of your hands, I find you, my seabed, my rock and my place of rest.

August 16th

Out of the depths I cry to you, O Lord,
Lord hear my voice!
O let your ears be attentive
to the voice of my pleading.

(Psalm 130:1–2)

At the depths of our greatest griefs and needs we will also find the seeds of our deepest trust and faith, hidden in our darkness.

August 17th

You have made the earth quake, torn it open.
Repair what is shattered, for it sways.
You have inflicted hardships on your people
and made us drink a wine that dazed us.

(Psalm 60:2–3)

Drunk with our illusions, and high on the drug of our own self-sufficiency, we stagger through the tumbling structures of our world. Yet there is still just enough vision left to show us our plight and our need, and to give voice to our cry to you for rescue.

August 18th

A remnant shall go out from Jerusalem,
and survivors from Mount Zion.
The love of the Lord shall accomplish this.

(2 Kings 19:31)

The seamless garment of your Kingdom is not made from
the finest rolls of fabric, but from the scraps and remnants
of faith that you have gathered from your people through
the ages and made one in your love.

August 19th

*'Beware of false prophets who come to you
disguised as sheep but underneath are ravenous
wolves. You will be able to tell them by their fruits.
Can people pick grapes from thorns, or figs from
thistles? In the same way, a sound tree produces
good fruit but a rotten tree bad fruit.'*

(Matthew 7:15–18)

The creatures of the woodland know how to distinguish between the colourful, seductive toadstools and the humble, hidden mushrooms, because they have noticed their effects. Lord, please give us the same wisdom in our lives and in our world.

August 20th

> *'Therefore, everyone who listens to these words of*
> *mine and acts on them will be like a sensible man*
> *who built his house on rock. Rain came down, floods*
> *rose, gales blew and hurled themselves against that*
> *house, and it did not fall: it was founded on rock.'*

(Matthew 7:24–26)

We place our trust in our homes and our jobs and our investments, yet the storms of recession or of war dissolve them in flash floods of destruction. And when all is gone, we find nothing but the hard rock, and the shocked realisation that only that Rock is able to hold us.

August 21st

By the rivers of Babylon
there we sat and wept, remembering Zion ...
O how could we sing the song of the Lord
on alien soil?

(Psalm 137:1, 4)

Yet when we find the heart to sing your song in a world
that rejects you, then our little patch of alien soil becomes
your home again, and a place where others might find you.

August 22nd

And going into Peter's house Jesus found Peter's mother-in-law in bed with fever. He touched her hand and the fever left her, and she got up and began to wait on him.

(Matthew 8:14–15)

You touch us with your love and the fever of our lives subsides. Our hearts become whole again, able to respond to you in joyful service.

And Jesus began to speak, first of all to his disciples:
'Be on your guard against the yeast of the Pharisees –
that is, their hypocrisy. Everything that is now hidden
will be made clear. For this reason, whatever you have
said in the dark will be heard in the daylight, and
what you have whispered in hidden places will be
proclaimed on the housetops.'

(Luke 12:1–3)

One worm can make the apple bad. One grain of yeast can make the loaf rise. Our lies can multiply into a torrent of evil, but our truth can swell the ocean of redeeming love.

August 24th

*Without warning a storm broke over the lake,
so violent that the waves were breaking right over
the boat. But Jesus was asleep. So they went to
him and woke him saying, 'Save us, Lord, we
are going down.'*

(Matthew 8:23–25)

Jennie came crying to her mother in the middle of the
night, to be comforted from the nightmare. A more
independent child – or one less loved – might have
struggled on alone, suppressing the terror, and never
known the calming reassurance of the loving presence of
one who was always there for her.

Let me have no more of the din of your chanting,
no more of your strumming on harps.
But let justice flow like water,
and integrity like an unfailing stream.

(Amos 5:23–24)

Not the justice that merely shouts from the soapbox, but that which flows quietly through all our daily dealings. Not the exhortations to be sinless, but the opportunities to be kind. Your grace, Lord, not our efforts.

August 26th

Then some people appeared, bringing him a
paralytic stretched out on a bed. Seeing their faith,
Jesus said to the paralytic 'Courage, my child,
your sins are forgiven.'

(Matthew 9:1–2)

When we are paralysed by the knowledge of our own
failures and fears, you free us by giving us the courage to
acknowledge our need and let you gently lift the crippling
burdens of the past from our hearts.

August 27th

*See what days are coming – it is the Lord who
speaks – days when I will bring a famine on the
country, a famine not of bread, a drought not of water,
but of hearing the word of the Lord. They will stagger
from sea to sea, wander from north to east, seeking
the word of the Lord and failing to find it.*

(Amos 8:11–12)

Lord, we are one with your staggering, wandering people,
but we carry your living water in our hearts to quench
their parching need, because we are also one with *you*.

August 28th

May he enlighten the eyes of your mind so that you
can see what hope his call holds for you.

(Ephesians 1:18)

The light of your hope, like the light of the stars, shines
most clearly through the deepest darkness. It may seem
so distant, yet it is the truest beacon and companion of
our night.

August 29th

*One of the scribes then came up and said to him,
'Master, I will follow you wherever you go.' Jesus
replied, 'Foxes have holes and the birds of the air
have nests, but the Son of Man has nowhere
to lay his head.'*

(Luke 9:57–58)

There are moments of desolation when there is no-one,
nowhere to turn to, and every direction seems to lead to
despair. And there, at the still centre of the storm, the
homeless One is waiting.

August 30th

Then he told them a parable: 'There was once a rich man who, having a good harvest from his land, thought to himself "What am I to do? I have not enough room to store my crops." Then he said: "This is what I will do: I will pull down my barns and build bigger ones, and store all my grain and my goods in them." … But God said to him "Fool! This very night the demand will be made for your soul; and this hoard of yours, whose will it be then?" '

(Luke 12:16–19, 20–21)

Jane worked tirelessly for charity, raising funds and stirring people into action. She committed more and more of her time and energy to this all-consuming passion. By the time she got to bed each night she was too exhausted to hear the sobbing of her little son, lying alone with his fears in the next room.

August 31st

However great the number of sins committed,
grace was even greater.

(Romans 5:20)

We try to carry your grace up the mountains of our lives
like a litre of water in a plastic bottle, and we pass by the
streams of your living spirit unnoticed and untasted.

SEPTEMBER

September 1st

Our life, like a bird, has escaped from the snare
of the fowler. Indeed the snare has been broken
and we have escaped.

(Psalm 124:7–8)

When I receive your gift of freedom, Lord, do I let its power carry me on eagle's wings, or do I tremble at the cage door like a stranded budgerigar, unable to risk a life beyond captivity?

September 2nd

*We are God's work of art, created in Christ Jesus
to love the good life as from the beginning
he had meant us to live it.*

(Ephesians 2:10)

The old painting had been buried in the vaults for long
forgotten years, yet in the hands of the restorers it was
cleansed and re-created until the full glory of the artist's
first intention shone from the canvas. It was a unique
expression of his mind and heart, and the world had been
incomplete without it.

September 3rd

*He is the peace between us ... In his own person
he killed the hostility.*

(Ephesians 2:14)

May we kill nothing except that which kills the wholeness
of each other. May we destroy nothing except the barriers
that divide us.

September 4th

*'No-one puts new wine into old wineskins; if they do,
the skins burst, the wine runs out, and the skins are
lost. No, they put new wine into fresh skins and
both are preserved.'*

(Matthew 9:17)

The first moments of life are the most hazardous, as old
and safe containers are left behind to make space for all
that is new. The risk of letting go is the price of life
and growth.

September 5th

*When he had reached a certain place, Jacob passed the
night there, since the sun had set. Taking one of the
stones to be found at that place, he made it his pillow
and lay down where he was. He had a dream:
a ladder was there, standing on the ground with its
top reaching to heaven, and there were angels of God
going up it and coming down. And the Lord was
there, standing over him … Jacob awoke from his
sleep and said: 'Truly, the Lord is in this place
and I never knew it.'*

(Genesis 28:10–17)

Between the stones of our despair we catch a glimpse of
the diamonds of your presence and your love, in the place
where we never thought to find you.

September 6th

Whatever you eat, whatever you drink, whatever you
do at all, do it for the glory of God.

(1 Corinthians 10:31)

Jane had always placed an extra chair at the table to remind her family of Jesus, 'the unseen guest at every meal'. Years later, in her final hours, she smiled across towards the empty chair beside her hospital bed, and the nurses noticed her face become radiant with a beauty not her own, as she closed her eyes in death.

September 7th

*'Do not worry about how to speak or what to say;
what you are to say will be given to you when
the time comes; because it is not you who will be
speaking; the Spirit of your Father will be speaking
in you.'*

(Matthew 10:19–20)

He was renowned for his talks and lectures, and the hall
was packed with people who had come a long way to hear
him. A cold shudder ran through him as he realised that he
had left his notes at home. He panicked for a moment, but
then steadied himself, in a few moments of prayerful calm,
before walking into the auditorium. Afterwards they said
that it was the best talk he had ever given.

September 8th

'What I say to you in the dark, tell in the daylight;
what you hear in whispers, proclaim from
the housetops.'

(Matthew 10:27)

What is given in the dark silence of prayer is for carrying
out into the bright lights and clamour of every day, for the
transforming of our lived experience.

September 9th

It is the Lord who speaks:
I am going to lure her
and lead her into the wilderness
and speak to her heart.

(Hosea 2:14)

When we are walking through the desert spaces in our lives and the searing sun is burning away all our masks and our defences – there, where nothing comes between us, we meet you face to face and you speak to our hearts.

September 10th

*And when Jesus saw the crowds he felt sorry for them
because they were harassed and dejected, like sheep
without a shepherd. Then he said to his disciples,
'The harvest is rich but the labourers are few, so
ask the Lord of the harvest to send labourers
to this harvest.'*

(Matthew 9:36–38)

The fields of my life are rich with the harvest of gifts you
have planted uniquely in my heart. Yet if I fail to gather in
their fruits and share them with a hungry world, you will
have planted them in vain.

Sow integrity for yourselves,
reap a harvest of kindness,
break up your fallow ground:
it is time to go seeking the Lord
until he comes to rain salvation on you.

(Hosea 10:12)

Katy had lived a good and law-abiding life, yet when she looked back there seemed little to show for it. Then came the ground-breaking years, when unseen stirrings shook her life's soil apart. The waiting time was yielding to the coming of the harvest, and she knew that it was time to seek the Lord in the hidden roots of her being.

September 12th

I will heal their disloyalty,
I will love them with all my heart,
for my anger has turned from them.
I will fall like dew on Israel.
He shall bloom like the lily
and thrust out roots like the poplar,
his shoots will spread far.

(Hosea 14:5–7)

When the waves of anger and resentment recede, then I shall see the firm sands and solid rock of love. And there I learn that what I resent, I hold captive, and am myself enslaved by it. What I learn to love I set free for growth and fruitfulness and am myself made fruitful by it.

September 13th

Then I heard the voice of the Lord saying:
'Whom shall I send? Who will be our messenger?'
I answered, 'Here I am, send me.'

(Isaiah 6:8)

Barbara was terrified of driving, but when her neighbour
had an accident she forgot her fear and drove him through
the rush-hour traffic to the hospital. There had been no
time to spare for asking: 'Who will drive?' There had only
been time to make the instant response of love.

September 14th

*John in his prison had heard what Christ was doing
and he sent his disciples to ask him, 'Are you the one
who is to come, or have we got to wait for someone
else?' Jesus answered, 'Go back and tell John what
you hear and see; the blind see again, and the lame
walk, lepers are cleansed and the deaf hear, and the
dead are raised to life and the Good News is
proclaimed to the poor.'*

(Matthew 11:2–6)

When we see the life-giving power of your healing in our
lives, we do not need to ask who you are.

September 15th

I have sunk into the mud of the deep
and there is no foothold.
I have entered the waters of the deep
and the waves overwhelm me.
This is my prayer to you, my prayer for your favour
In your great love, answer me, O God,
with your help that never fails.

(Psalm 69:2–4)

At the bottom of the deepest layer of mud there will be the solid rock that will hold me and let me fall no further. I know it from my experience. Why do I always forget it while I am sinking?

September 16th

You shall eat the Passover like this: with a girdle round your waist, sandals on your feet, a staff in your hand. You shall eat it hastily; it is a passover in honour of the Lord.

(Exodus 11:11)

The journey is unfinished, and you call us, your Passover people, to be always ready for the onward road, every communion with you a preparation for moving on.

September 17th

*'When a man has had a great deal given him, a great
deal will be demanded of him.'*

(Luke 12:48)

Diane knew that the brightest and most gifted children in
her class of eight-year-olds could be prone to boredom, so
she sometimes asked them to help the slower ones with
their reading and writing. They passed their own skills on
to their classmates, and in return they learned patience and
responsibility. It was a sharing of gifts which helped to
change the class into a real community.

September 18th

'You know how to interpret the face of the earth and the sky. How is it you do not know how to interpret these times?'

(Luke 12:56)

We are so immersed in the laboratory of human knowledge that we sometimes forget to look out of the window and see what is actually happening to us. Lord, take our knowledge, and transform it into wisdom.

September 19th

Pay attention, keep calm, have no fear,
do not let your heart sink.

(Isaiah 7:4)

When my heart sinks, it sinks into the quicksands of my own fears and pre-occupations, where it can see nothing except itself. When I lift it up to you, it rises into freedom, where it can see your world and your suffering children.

September 20th

Jesus exclaimed, 'I bless you, Father, Lord of heaven and of earth, for hiding these things from the learned and the clever and revealing them to mere children.'

(Matthew 11:25)

Underneath all the layers of our learning and our skills lies a heart that once knew how to marvel at the simple miracle of life – a heart that once received life without needing to conquer or control it, and a heart that can still recapture that first dawn of wonder.

September 21st

As a woman with child near her time
writhes and cries out in her prayer,
so are we, O Lord, in your presence.
We have conceived, we writhe
as if we were giving birth.

(Isaiah 26:17–18)

Once your love has been conceived in our hearts we have
no choice but to bring it to birth in our world. We con-
sented to the conception, Lord, and we consent to the
pains of labour, for the sake of the coming of your
Kingdom.

September 22nd

If we live by the truth and in love,
we shall grow in all ways into Christ.

(Ephesians 4:16)

When we live out the dream you have planted in our hearts, discerning it gradually in the light of your truth and your love, then we shall become who you are calling us to be, as surely as the acorn becomes an oak.

September 23rd

Woe to those who plot evil,
who lie in bed planning mischief!
No sooner is it dawn than they do it.

(Micah 2:1)

When we lie and brood in our own inner darkness, our worst fears take us over and our worst intentions can become reality. But when we surrender ourselves to you in the dark silence of prayer, your joy can become incarnate, and your dream can come to fulfilment.

September 24th

*'The kingdom of heaven is like a mustard seed which
a man took and sowed in his field. It is the smallest of
all the seeds, but when it has grown it is the biggest
shrub of all and becomes a tree so that the birds of the
air come and shelter in its branches.'*

(Matthew 13:31–32)

When we see the complex creatures that we are, we know
that each of us began as just a single cell. When we see the
microscopic single cell of our faith, we wonder what it
might become.

September 25th

The pillar of cloud would come down and station itself
at the entrance to the Tent, and the Lord would speak
with Moses ... The Lord would speak with Moses
face to face, as a man speaks with his friend.

(Exodus 33:9, 11)

The man called to lead his people to freedom is the man
who knows God in the intimacy of friendship.

September 26th

> *Jesus addressed the lawyers and Pharisees, 'Is it*
> *against the law,' he asked, 'to cure a man on the*
> *sabbath, or not?' But they remained silent, so he took*
> *the man and cured him and sent him away. Then he*
> *said to them, 'Which of you here, if his son falls into*
> *a well, or his ox, will not pull him out on a sabbath*
> *day without hesitation?' And to this they could find*
> *no answer.*

(Luke 14:3–6)

The demands of love always take precedence over the
demands of law. They are the demands of our hearts and of
God's, to which there can be no other answer.

September 27th

'Everyone who exalts himself will be humbled,
and the man who humbles himself will be exalted.'

(Luke 14:11)

Queues of tourists wait in line to visit the palace.
Tomorrow their day will be just a fading memory. Once it
was the other way round, and kings lined up to visit a
stable. We are still talking about their visit two thousand
years later.

September 28th

During the celebrations for Herod's birthday, the daughter of Herodias danced before the company and so delighted Herod that he promised on oath to give her anything she asked. Prompted by her mother she said, 'Give me John the Baptist's head, here, on a dish.' The king was distressed, but, thinking of the oaths he had sworn and of his guests, he ordered it to be given her, and sent and had John beheaded in the prison.

(Matthew 14:6–10)

He had had too much to drink and was in no mood to be coaxed home by his embarrassed wife. Instead he told a crude story against her. His pride was saved, but something irreplaceable was lost, that evening.

September 29th

This is what the Lord asks of you:
only this, to act justly,
to love tenderly
and to walk humbly with your God.

(Micah 6:8)

When we walk humbly with you, we cannot fail to be touched by your tenderness, and when your tender love has touched us, truth and justice are our only options.

September 30th

*Jesus was teaching in one of the synagogues, and a
woman was there who for eighteen years had been
possessed by a spirit that left her enfeebled; she was
bent double and quite unable to stand upright. When
Jesus saw her, he called her over ... and he laid his
hands on her. And at once she straightened up, and
she glorified God.*

(Luke 13:10–13)

Mark would never have claimed to have a gift of healing;
but he knew when one of the children in his care was
crushed by a burden of self-doubt and inadequacy, and he
knew how to nurture the crippled little sapling into a tall,
straight tree.

OCTOBER

October 1st

Before I formed you in the womb I knew you;
before you came to birth, I consecrated you.

(Jeremiah 1:5)

Bernard grew prize gladioli. Each year he lovingly planted the bulbs, and for every bulb he planted he had a vision in his heart of the perfect flower it would become, nurtured by him until it should reveal the fullness of its still-hidden mystery.

October 2nd

My people have abandoned me,
the fountain of living water,
only to dig cisterns for themselves,
leaky cisterns, that hold no water.

(Jeremiah 2:13)

For years I used all my energy in trying to dig my own wells of wisdom. When I returned to you, defeated and exhausted, I found, once more, the spring of living water, undiminished and unpolluted, freely given and effortlessly received.

October 3rd

The one who received the seed in rich soil is the
person who hears the word and understands it;
he is the one who yields a harvest.

(Matthew 13:23)

The yield of the harvest lies not in the labour of our
hands, but in the receptiveness of our hearts.

October 4th

*'The kingdom of heaven may be compared to a man
who sowed good seed in his field. While everyone was
asleep his enemy came, sowed darnel all among the
wheat, and made off. When the new wheat sprouted
and ripened, the darnel appeared as well. The owner's
servants went to him and said: "Sir, was it not good
seed that you sowed in your field? If so, where does
the darnel come from?" "Some enemy has done this,"
he answered.'*

(Matthew 13:24–28)

Like weeds, my persistent fears grow fast and furious,
taking over my mind and my heart. Yet it is the sure and
steady growth of joy that will have the final word; the
good seed of joy that is the original inhabitant and right-
ful heir of my life's soil, and will be its eternal harvest.

October 5th

They fashioned a calf at Horeb
and worshipped an image of metal,
exchanging the God who was their glory
for the image of a bull that eats grass.

(Psalm 106:19–20)

James was a self-made man. He had a successful career, a well-organised family and a tidy, prosperous lifestyle. Self-made, from head to toe, but unable to face the empty space where God had intended his heart to be.

October 6th

I am quite certain that the One who began this good work in you will see that it is finished when the Day of Christ Jesus comes.

(Philippians 1:6)

The One who caused all creation to grow from a single spark of life will surely grow his seed in us to the fullness of its blossom and its fruitfulness.

October 7th

The king said to his servants, 'The wedding is ready;
but as those who were invited proved to be unworthy,
go to the crossroads in the town and invite everyone
you can find to the wedding.' So these servants went
out onto the roads and collected together everyone they
could find, bad and good alike, and the wedding hall
was filled with guests.

(Matthew 22:8–10)

We may be very surprised when we see some of the
unlikely people you have invited to your wedding feast –
but they may be even more surprised if they find *us* there!

October 8th

*As Jesus drew near Jerusalem and came in sight of the
city he shed tears over it and said: 'If you in your turn
had only understood on this day the message of peace!
But, alas, it is hidden from your eyes! ... and all
because you did not recognise your opportunity when
God offered it!'*

(Luke 19:41–42, 44)

The phone call came a few moments too late. The car
wouldn't start. There was a hold-up on the motorway. By
the time he rushed into the intensive care unit his brother
had just died. The word of forgiveness would never be
spoken ... Never again ... His heart cracked ... if only!

October 9th

When you enter the land that I give you, and
gather in the harvest there, you must bring the first
sheaf of your harvest to the priest, and he is to present
it to the Lord.

(Leviticus 23:10–11)

You give me all the gifts of my life, and to you I return
them, for you know far better than I how they might best
be used.

October 10th

Naaman the leper went down and immersed himself
seven times in the Jordan, as Elisha had told him to
do. And his flesh became clean once more like the flesh
of a child. Returning to Elisha, he said 'Now I know
that there is no God in all the earth except in Israel.
Now please accept a present from your servant.' But
Elisha replied, 'As the Lord lives, whom I serve,
I will accept nothing.'

(2 Kings 5:14–16)

There is nothing we can give you in gratitude for our
healing, except to live out the fullness of lives made whole
again, as reflections of your love.

October 11th

*'The kingdom of heaven is like the yeast a woman
took and mixed in with three measures of flour till it
was leavened all through.'*

(Matthew 13:33)

A teaspoon of the yeast of *your* kingdom can leaven a
whole lifetime of the dough of mine.

October 12th

If I go into the countryside,
there lie men killed by the sword;
if I go into the city,
I see people sick with hunger ...
O God, you are our hope.

(Jeremiah 14:18, 22)

Our pangs of hunger make us seek out the food we need; our pains cause us to look for healing; our anger makes us work for justice and our encounters with evil set us journeying in search of our redeeming.

October 13th

'The kingdom of heaven is like a merchant looking for fine pearls; when he finds one of great value he goes and sells everything he owns and buys it.'

(Matthew 13:45–46)

The deepest desire of my heart is the one that I will follow, letting go of all the lesser ones. Will it lead me to the fullness of your kingdom, or to the bankruptcy of my own?

October 14th

So I went down to the potter's house; and there he
was, working at the wheel. And whenever the vessel he
was making came out wrong, he would start afresh
and work it into another vessel, as potters do …
As the clay is in the potter's hand, so you are
in mine.

(Jeremiah 18:1–6)

We are held in hands that assure us that every false start is
a new beginning and every failure an opportunity for a
new creation.

October 15th

*'Where did the man get this wisdom and these
miraculous powers? This is the carpenter's son, surely.'*

(Matthew 13:54-55)

We strain our eyes to see miracles on our life's horizon,
and fail to see them lying on the doorstep of our own
experience.

October 16th

The Lord listens to the needy
and does not spurn his servants in their chains.

(Psalm 69:33)

Our circumstances hold us captive, as a fence surrounds a field. Yet we have the choice, to focus our gaze on the fence that encloses us or on the view that our field affords, on the clamour of our needs, or on the Lord who listens.

October 17th

When we brought the Good News to you, it came to you not only as words, but as power and as the Holy Spirit and as utter conviction.

(1 Thessalonians 1:4–5)

Janice rarely speaks directly of her faith. But in the quiet authority of the life she lives in you, those who know her know that they are touching one who is in touch with you, one through whom the currents of your love are flowing.

October 18th

Jesus went towards them, walking on the water ...
He called out to them saying 'Courage! It is I.
Do not be afraid.' It was Peter who answered, 'Lord,'
he said, 'if it is you, tell me to come to you across the
water.' 'Come,' said Jesus. Then Peter got out of the
boat and started walking towards Jesus across the
water, but as soon as he felt the force of the wind
he took fright and began to sink.

(Matthew 14:25–30)

Philip was well in the lead and seemed certain to win the race. All his energy was focused on that one supreme goal. Then there was a disturbance among the spectators. He glanced sideways at the crowd, suddenly conscious of his surroundings and their dangers. From that moment his focus was lost, and so was the race.

October 19th

*At the end of forty days they came back from the
reconnaissance of the land ... They told them this
story, 'We went into the land to which you sent us.
It does indeed flow with milk and honey; this is its
produce. At the same time its inhabitants are a
powerful people.'*

(Numbers 13:25–28)

Just when I begin to taste the joy of the milk and the
honey, I come face to face with one of the powerful giants
of fear, or doubt, or pride, who populate my inner kingdom. The honey of your promise is not drawn from a bed
of roses.

October 20th

The Lord is your guard and your shade;
at your right side he stands.
By day the sun shall not smite you,
nor the moon in the night.

(Psalm 121:5–6)

In those parts of our life that seem like empty deserts, we feel the extremes of the desert climate: the burning pain of anger or disappointment; the cold darkness of despair. But you, who made both sun and moon, hold us in the far greater orbit of your unchanging love.

October 21st

How rich are the depths of God – how deep his
wisdom and knowledge – and how impossible to
penetrate his motives or understand his methods!
Who could ever know the mind of the Lord?
Who could ever be his counsellor?

(Romans 11:33–35)

Your wisdom rises beyond us as the stars above the highest mountain peak. Yet still, Lord, we try to advise you on how to arrange your world and the details of our little lives. Still we try to capture the vastness of your purpose within the cramped cages of our minds.

October 22nd

Moses said to the people: 'Listen, Israel: the Lord our
God is the one Lord. You shall love the Lord your
God with all your heart, with all your soul, with all
your strength. Let these words I urge on you today be
written on your heart. You shall fasten them on your
hand and on your forehead; you shall write them on
the doorposts of your house.'

(Deuteronomy 6:4–9)

Sue and David's home is always open. All sorts of people
seek them out and find a welcome there. If you could see
into the deep recesses of their being, you would find these
words inscribed on the doorposts of their hearts: 'God lives
here.'

October 23rd

All of us, in union with Christ, form one body,
and as parts of it we belong to each other.

(Romans 12:5–6)

We stand together, each one a link in the circle of life, each *needing* our neighbours, each *holding* our neighbours, and all held in God.

October 24th

The Lord leaned down from his sanctuary on high.
He looked down from heaven to the earth
that he might hear the groans of the prisoners
and free those condemned to die.

(Psalm 102:19–20)

You do not hear our groanings from somewhere high above us, Lord, or even from alongside us, but from right inside us, inside the locked cells of our hearts and holding the key to our freedom.

October 25th

They have found pardon in the wilderness,
those who have survived the sword.

(Jeremiah 31:2)

The quarrel with his former friend left Richard devastated
and inwardly bleeding. For months he existed in an inner
desert. Only two things grew in that desert. One was the
choking tangle of his remorse and his regrets. The other
was the soft, determined flower of your forgiveness and
your peace.

October 26th

You must love your neighbour as yourself. Love is the one thing that cannot hurt your neighbour; that is why it is the answer to every one of the commandments.

(Romans 13:9–10)

But love can hurt the one who gives it. Love brings us up against our most painful choices. Love strips away our masks and exposes our deepest truth. And precisely because of that, love heals.

October 27th

*'What, then, will a man gain if he wins the whole
world and ruins his life? Or what has a man to offer
in exchange for his life?'*

(Matthew 16:25–26)

Let our energies be spent for living, and not for building
up mere monuments to life.

October 28th

*'The man who can be trusted in little things can be
trusted in great; the man who is dishonest in little
things will be dishonest in great.'*

(Luke 16:10–11)

If I can trust you with the burdens of my heart, I do not
need to wonder whether I can trust you with the contents
of my purse.

October 29th

Let everything that lives and breathes
give praise to the Lord. Alleluia!

(Psalm 150:6)

Remind us, Lord, that when we walk through our gardens and along our streets, we are moving through a hallowed cathedral where there is always a service in progress.

October 30th

I rejoiced when I heard them say
'Let us go to God's house.'
And now our feet are standing
within your gates, O Jerusalem.

(Psalm 122:1–2)

Prayer begins with the first quiver of desire to spend time in your presence, and before I know what has happened I am a guest in your heart and a pilgrim in your Kingdom.

October 31st

Jar of meal shall not be spent,
jug of oil shall not be emptied,
before the day when the Lord sends rain
on the face of the earth.

(1 Kings 17:14)

When we come to the last remnants of our own resources,
we are standing close to the brink of your saving grace.

NOVEMBER

November 1st

Cure the sick, raise the dead, cleanse the lepers,
cast out devils. You received without charge, give
without charge.

(Matthew 10:8)

A gentle touch on a fevered forehead.
A warm greeting to raise dead spirits back to hope.
An embrace of acceptance for the unlovely.
A word of affirmation to cast out fear.
All freely given, and asking nothing more of us but that we
freely pass them on.

November 2nd

Jesus said: 'This is what the kingdom of God is like.
A man throws seed on the land. Night and day, while
he sleeps, when he is awake, the seed is sprouting and
growing; how, he does not know.'

(Mark 4:26–28)

The seed of your kingdom lives and grows more freely in
the heart of a sleeping child, than in all the collected works
of the world's theologians. Let us not ask to know how. Let
us simply be the soil for your seeding.

November 3rd

*'It was good of you to share with me in my
hardships … It is not your gift that I value;
what is valuable to me is the interest that is
mounting up in your account.'*

(Philippians 4:14, 17)

You invest the capital of your love in our hearts, Lord, and
the more we draw upon it, the more interest you pay us.

November 4th

'Why, every hair on your head has been counted.
So there is no need to be afraid.'

(Matthew 10:31)

Joan held her new-born daughter in her arms, stroking each toe and finger and caressing the tiny eyebrows with a love that would spend itself gladly, in the years to come, for the one who had come to birth. Do you not hold us, too, in tenderness, Lord, and spend yourself in love for us? You, who are the source and well-spring of all our loving.

November 5th

'Peace I bequeath to you, my own peace I give you, a peace which the world cannot give is my gift to you.'

(John 14:27)

The deepest part of us, that dwells in you, remains at peace whatever storms are raging in our lives. Help us, Lord, to find that deep centre of stillness in you where we draw the strength and the courage of your peace in all our life's circumstances.

November 6th

'You have shown you can be faithful in small things,
I will trust you with greater; come and join in
your master's happiness.'

(Matthew 25:21)

Ruth had been hurt that day in the office, many years ago, by the unjust reprimand, and Elaine had helped to ease the hurt by resting her hand on her colleague's arm in a gesture of understanding. Today, as Ruth reeled under the shock of the diagnosis of her terminal illness, she remembered that gesture of love, and suddenly she knew who to turn to in her need and her loneliness.

November 7th

'Come to me, all you who labour and are over-
burdened, and I will give you rest. Shoulder my yoke
and learn from me, for I am gentle and humble in
heart and you will find rest for your souls. Yes, my
yoke is easy and my burden light.'

(Matthew 11:28–30)

We find your promised rest, not by evading the burdens of
our lives, but by carrying them in your strength. We find
our deepest freedom when we are yoked to you.

November 8th

*Jesus said to them: 'A prophet is only despised in his
own country, among his own relatives and in his own
house,' and he could work no miracles there, though he
cured a few sick people by laying his hands on them.
He was amazed at their lack of faith.*

(Mark 6:4–6)

Suppose, Lord, that you were to walk among us now,
among those who call themselves your own friends,
brothers and sisters, and suppose you were to walk through
your own house here in our town today ... would you
find among us the faith that would open the path of your
transforming power to our world, or would you shake
your head and sadly walk away?

November 9th

'I am sending you out like lambs among wolves.
Carry no purse, no haversack, no sandals.
Salute no-one on the road. Whatever house you go
into, let your first words be: "Peace on this house!"
And if a man of peace lives there, your peace will go
and rest on him.'

(Luke 10:4–7)

The market place is milling with Saturday shoppers. Occasionally I look into the face of a passing stranger and her glance meets mine. For a second or two a shaft of recognition passes between us, and we know we have met momentarily in our shared humanity and been enriched by that meeting as we pass on our separate ways. Our peace has rested upon each other and been received.

November 10th

*The learned will shine as brightly as the vault of
heaven, and those who have instructed many in virtue,
as bright as stars for all eternity.*

(Daniel 12:3)

When we hold our children in our arms, gently pointing
out the consequences of hurting others, the light we
kindle in their minds casts its glow over all the human
family.

November 11th

The Lord turns his face against the wicked
to destroy their remembrance from the earth.
The Lord turns his eyes to the just
and his ears to their appeal.

(Psalm 34:15–16)

It had been a grim sort of a day. As she climbed into bed, Jean nearly sank under the depressing weight of a series of mistakes, misjudgements and harsh, unnecessary words. But there had been that moment of kindness from a passing stranger, which had made her feel more kindly to her fellow human beings, and there had been that new shoot on the camellia bush, which had made her feel more kindly to herself. She switched off the light and let the destructive things fade out of remembrance, and turned her eyes instead to those moments of light.

November 12th

*The day is coming now, burning like a furnace; and
all the arrogant and evil-doers will be like stubble. The
day that is coming is going to burn them up, says the
Lord of hosts, leaving them neither root nor stalk. But
for you who fear my name, the sun of righteousness
will shine out with healing in its rays.*

(Malachi 3:19–20)

Out of the harvest of our lives, the stubble of our failure.
Out of the stubble of failure, the smoke of our shame. Out
of the smoke of shame, the ashes of hope, and out of the
ashes the nutrients for the new life, waiting for the healing
rays of the sun, and a new beginning.

November 13th

Those who are sowing in tears
will sing when they reap.
They go out, they go out, full of tears,
carrying seed for the sowing:
they come back, they come back, full of song,
carrying their sheaves.

(Psalm 126:6)

The grey, wintry sky depressed Jake as he seeded the crop, his skin gradually soaking up the cold, seeping drizzle. Somewhere in his memory was the dream of a harvest supper, but it seemed a long way off. At home his wife was struggling to persuade their baby to eat his meal. Her frustration all but smothered her hopes for the full-grown son he would become. Then evening came, and they sat beside the fire, and silently warmed their dreams together.

November 14th

For I, the Lord, your God,
I am holding you by the right hand;
I tell you, 'Do not be afraid, I will help you.'

(Isaiah 41:13)

Everyone could hear the hysterical sobbing amid the crowd of Christmas shoppers, but no-one could quite see where it was coming from. Then the child's mother made her way through the mass of people, gently, but with firm determination. She reached out to take hold of her toddler's hand. At once the sobbing stopped, and all was well.

November 15th

Give your servant a heart to understand how to discern between good and evil.

(1 Kings 3:9)

Decisions may be made in my head, but discernment can only happen in my heart.

November 16th

There is one Body, one Spirit, just as you were all
called into one and the same hope when you were
called. There is one Lord, one faith, one baptism,
and one God who is Father of all, through all
and within all.

(Ephesians 4:4–6)

Our divisions are like the fences we might erect to mark
the boundaries of our human territories. Below the fences
lies the soil in which all our hearts are rooted, and below
the soil is the rock upon which all our faith is founded.

November 17th

*'What father among you would hand his son a stone
when he asked for bread? Or hand him a snake
instead of a fish? Or hand him a scorpion if he
asked for an egg? If you, who are evil, know how
to give your children what is good, how much more
will the heavenly Father give the Holy Spirit to those
who ask him?'*

(Luke 11:11–13)

Alice was dying before her time, in a makeshift hospital
ward at the end of the war. A minor operation had gone
wrong because she was so weakened by hunger. Yet there
was joy in her eyes as she held her little grandson in her
arms. Then she pressed a small paper bag into his hands –
her month's sugar ration and her only source of energy. A
small token of immeasurable love.

November 18th

*Moses said to the people: 'Love the stranger then, for
you were strangers in the land of Egypt.'*

(Deuteronomy 10:19)

The children stood round in a huddle and stared at the
newcomer, as he trailed shyly, fearfully, across the playground. It was Martin who broke the wall of tension with
a friendly word for the frightened stranger. Martin had
been new here himself last term.

November 19th

*Jesus called a little child to him and set the child in
front of him. Then he said: 'I tell you solemnly, unless
you change and become like little children you will
never enter the kingdom of heaven. And so, the one
who makes himself as little as this little child is the
greatest in the kingdom of heaven.'*

(Matthew 18:2–4)

The Reception Class is well named. It is not only the place
for those who are to be received, but also for those who,
of all people, are the ones most receptive to the wonders
that lie around them, waiting for discovery.

November 20th

*Asked by the Pharisees when the kingdom of God
was to come, Jesus gave them this answer, 'The coming
of the kingdom of God does not admit of observation
and there will be no-one to say, "Look here! Look
there!" For, you must know, the kingdom of God is
among you.'*

(Luke 17:20–22)

Hour by hour your Kingdom comes, silently, impercep-
tibly, powerfully as springtime, with all the fragile
determination of the butterfly emerging from the
caterpillar. We are called, not to watch anxiously for its
coming, but joyfully to recognise its ever-present reality.

November 21st

Joshua said to the Israelites: 'Come closer and hear the words of the Lord your God. By this you shall know that a living God is with you.'

(Joshua 3:10)

Jane's correspondence with her pen-friend had been, necessarily, a little forced and stilted. But when they finally met and stayed in each other's homes, their paper connection changed into a living relationship that was a source of richness and joy to them both. Help us to change our long-distance acquaintance with you into the close and living encounter you long for it to be.

November 22nd

> *'As the lightning flashing from one part of heaven
> lights up the other, so will be the Son of Man, when
> his day comes.'*
>
> (Luke 17:24–25)

It was impossible to pinpoint the source of the flash at the centre of the storm, but its invisible power lit up the fields and forests all around, revealing their every detail. And so the unseen flashpoint of your love lights up our darkest corners and kindles fire in our hearts, which glows and flares far beyond the limits of our own lives and our own imagination.

*I know all about you: how hard you work and how
much you put up with … Nevertheless I have this
complaint to make; you have less love now than you
used to. Think where you were before you fell;
repent and do as you used to at first.*

(Revelation 2:2, 4–5)

The home they had once built as a love-nest had become
a chore, and the garden had become a backache. The
children had become a worry and God had become a
Sunday observance. So much work; so much to put up
with – and underneath all that, there was *everything* waiting
for re-discovery.

November 24th

*I saw something that looked like the glory of the
Lord. I looked, and prostrated myself.*

(Ezekiel 1:28)

If I look back over each day's living, I will find a speck of
gold among the sand-grains, a moment in which I have
recognised your *I AM* in mine.

November 25th

The Lord said, 'Son of Man, eat what is given to
you; eat this scroll, then go and speak to the House
of Israel.' I opened my mouth; he gave me the scroll
to eat and said, 'Son of Man, feed and be satisfied
by the scroll I am giving you.' I ate it, and it tasted
sweet as honey.

(Ezekiel 3:1–3)

Your Word is not for filing in the reference sections of our
heads, but for taking into ourselves and digesting, and for
becoming the truth with which it feeds us.

November 26th

'If your brother does something wrong ... and if he
refuses to listen to the community, treat him like a
pagan or a tax collector.'

(Matthew 18:17)

... yet remembering, Lord, that you also treated the pagans
and the tax collectors with love.

November 27th

*'I cancelled all that debt of yours when you appealed
to me. Were you not bound, then, to have pity on your
fellow servant just as I had pity on you?'*

(Matthew 18:33)

Chris was amazed when his boss let him off so lightly after
he had messed up such an important contract through his
carelessness. The tension of the day was still driving him
when he arrived home and lashed out at his son for not
doing his homework conscientiously. It was only when he
lay in bed that night that he remembered the grace of the
day, and its shame.

November 28th

*With joy you will draw water from the wells
of salvation.*

(Isaiah 12:3)

The springs of grace that flow in the privacy of our hearts
are deeper than drought and pure beyond pollution.
Private wells, but flowing with a love for universal sharing.

November 29th

The upright man is law-abiding and honest: he does not seduce his neighbour's wife; he oppresses no-one, returns pledges, never steals, gives his own bread to the hungry, his clothes to the naked. He never charges usury on loans, takes no interest, abstains from evil, gives honest judgement between man and man, keeps my laws and sincerely respects my observances.

(Ezekiel 18:5–9)

You walked along the High Street, looking for an upright man. You stopped at the newsagents and noticed the magazines on the top shelf. You stopped by the homeless man crouched on a doorstep, and noticed us hurrying by. You stopped outside the bank and noticed the posters advertising bank loans and credit cards. Then you stopped by the school, and watched a mother lead her little child to safety through the hazards of the city traffic, and I knew that you had found what you were looking for.

November 30th

*You are a letter from Christ, written not with ink but
with the Spirit of the Living God; not on stone tablets
but on the tablets of human hearts.*

(2 Corinthians 3:2–3)

What kind of 'letter' will I be to those I meet today?
A threatening letter? An angry demand? A dutiful note?
Or a letter written in love?

DECEMBER

December 1st

Oh, House of Jacob, come,
let us walk in the light of the Lord.

(Isaiah 2:5)

I closed my book and turned out the light. It was then that I noticed the night sky, bright with starlight. As long as the light in my own room was burning, all I could see was my own room and its messy contents. But when I re-focused my gaze to what lay outside and beyond me, my vision was drawn out to a reality far beyond myself, and infinitely greater.

December 2nd

A voice cries in the wilderness:
prepare a way for the Lord,
make his paths straight.

(Mark 1:3)

In the good times, when my life's music is playing at top volume, I hear no voice except my own. But when I am lost and bewildered, a new voice breaks through into the wilderness of my heart, calling me to take just one next step along the path that leads me home.

December 3rd

We exult and we rejoice that he has saved us;
for the hand of the Lord rests on this mountain.

(Isaiah 25:9–10)

The mountain of anxieties and resistances in my heart and
in my life seemed insurmountable, until, in the quiet of
prayer, you rested your hand of blessing upon it. From then
on, however harsh the terrain, it became the mountain
where I had met *you,* and a place of joy and gratitude.

December 4th

Open to me the gates of holiness:
I will enter and give thanks.

(Psalm 118:19)

You open the gates of your presence to us in the separate-
ness and silence of our prayer, but when we go *through*
those gates, we find ourselves in the heart of the hurts and
the needs of our brothers and sisters.

December 5th

Every valley will be filled in,
every mountain and hill be laid low,
winding ways will be straightened
and rough roads made smooth.
And all mankind shall see the salvation of God.

(Luke 3:5–6)

When we come home to you, you will not look back and remind us of the years we have trudged up and down the hills and valleys of our griefs and joys. Nor will you reproach us for the detours we have followed, the signposts we have missed, the cul-de-sacs we have been trapped in. You will simply rejoice in our arrival and never let us be lost again.

December 6th

A man came, sent by God. His name was John.
He came as a witness, as a witness to speak for that
Light so that everyone might believe through him.
He was not the Light, only a witness to speak
for the Light.

(John 1:6–8)

We are not called to be lights ourselves, but to be the clear glass panes through which your light might shine on others.

December 7th

Some men appeared, carrying on a bed a paralysed
man whom they were trying to bring in and lay down
in front of Jesus. But as the crowd made it impossible
to find a way of getting him in, they went up on to
the flat roof and lowered him and his stretcher down
through the tiles into the middle of the gathering, in
front of Jesus.

(Luke 5:18–19)

With hindsight I can see that it was often when life 'let me down' that I found myself closest to you and your healing touch.

December 8th

*When the Lord has given you the bread of suffering
and the water of distress, he who is your teacher will
hide no longer, and you will see your teacher with
your own eyes ... he will send rain for the seed you
sow in the ground and the bread that the ground
provides will be rich and nourishing.*

(Isaiah 30:20, 23)

The bread that springs from the seeds of our sorrow will
sustain us more truly and more completely than the fairy
cakes of our fleeting pleasures.

December 9th

The mountains may depart,
the hills be shaken,
but my love for you will never leave you.

(Isaiah 54:10)

The earthquakes of our experience re-arrange the landscape of our lives, and the changing scenes give us ever-new possibilities to seek you and to find you.

December 10th

Thus says the Lord, your redeemer,
the Holy One of Israel:
'I, the Lord, your God,
teach you what is good for you,
I lead you in the way that you must go.'

(Isaiah 48:17)

In a world where every demand and pressure seems to *drive* us, may we know your love that *meets* us where we are, and *leads* us gently forwards towards our own deepest truth in you.

Send victory like a dew, you heavens,
and let the clouds rain it down.

(Isaiah 45:8)

The only victory that is worthy of a human heart is a victory that leaves gentleness and fruitful growth in its wake, not grief and mourning.

December 12th

The Lord is good and upright.
He shows the path to those who stray,
he guides the humble in the right path;
he teaches his way to the poor.

(Psalm 25:8–9)

The map was no use. The directions I had been given made no sense when I was lost. Then a friendly companion came alongside: 'I'll come with you and show you the way,' he said. And I knew that I had met you, my Lord and guide, in the maze of my life, and that your way of leading me is to walk the way *with* me.

December 13th

*Jesus spoke to the crowds: 'What description can I find
for this generation? It is like children shouting to each
other as they sit in the market place:
"We played the pipes for you and
you wouldn't dance;
We sang dirges and you wouldn't be mourners."'*

(Matthew 11:16–17)

I notice that my most desolate moods descend when the
world won't dance to my tune, or cry over my little trou-
bles, and that I feel most at peace when I am so absorbed
in the music, or the sorrow, of another that I forget to
think about my own.

December 14th

'If anyone has two tunics he must share with the man
who has none, and the one with something to eat
must do the same.'

(Luke 3:11)

The voice of the world says: multiply what you have;
the voice of the Lord says: divide what you have and share
   it with those who have not.
The voice of the world says: satisfy your hunger;
the voice of the Lord says: satisfy your neighbour's hunger.

The Lord is my light and my help;
whom shall I fear?
The Lord is the stronghold of my life;
before whom shall I shrink?

(Psalm 27:1)

When I stand in the full light of the noonday sun I do not worry about whether my torch battery might fail. Then, Lord, knowing you to be the ground of my being, may I let go of the many lesser matters that pull me down into anxiety?

December 16th

It is the Lord God who speaks,
who gathers the outcasts of Israel.

(Isaiah 56:8)

You draw to yourself the ones we push to the outside edges. You listen to the ones without a voice. You turn us inside out, to show us who we really are.

December 17th

May the mountains bring forth peace for the people,
and the hills justice.

(Psalm 72:3)

The most fertile soil in the area had its ancient origins in a volcanic eruption, which had brought devastation in its wake. So, too, Lord, our worst upheavals are often the source of our richest growth.

December 18th

*The angel of the Lord appeared to him in a dream
and said, 'Joseph son of David, do not be afraid to
take Mary home as your wife, because she has
conceived what is in her by the Holy Spirit.'*

(Matthew 1:20)

It frightens us too, Lord, and it can frighten those around
us, when your seed starts to grow in our hearts. Give us
the courage to embrace our deepest truths and take
them home.

December 19th

*'He will turn the hearts of fathers towards their
children and the disobedient back to the wisdom
that the virtuous have, preparing for the Lord
a people fit for him.'*

(Luke 1:17)

Turning back to you will always challenge us to turn back
to each other. There cannot be the one without the other.

December 20th

'I am the handmaid of the Lord,' said Mary,
'let what you have said be done to me.'

(Luke 1:38)

She gave you the blank cheque of her life. You cashed it in. You took everything she had, and more, and left her grieving at the foot of the cross. And then you returned her capital with so much interest that all the world could live on it from that day forward.

December 21st

'Know this, too: your kinswoman Elizabeth has, in
her old age, herself conceived a son, and she whom
people called barren is now in her sixth month, for
nothing is impossible to God.'

(Luke 1:36–37)

The most barren places of our experience are often preg-
nant with our deepest truths, if we will only wait and
watch, in patient trust, for their gestation.

December 22nd

As soon as Elizabeth heard Mary's greeting,
the child leapt in her womb and Elizabeth was filled
with the Holy Spirit.

(Luke 1:41)

When two or more of us come together in your name, your still-unborn presence in each of us causes your still-unborn self in every other to leap for joy.

December 23rd

Lord, make me know your ways.
Lord, teach me your paths.
Make me walk in your truth, and teach me.

(Psalm 25:4)

You do not call us to study your truth, or to understand it, explain it or teach it. You call us to *walk* in it until we know every contour of its landscape, to be at home in it, and to entrust each day's journey entirely to its leading. You call us to a knowledge that will be imprinted on the soles of our feet and etched in the hollows of our hearts.

December 24th

*'The maiden is with child and will soon give birth to
a son whom she will call Immanuel, a name which
means "God-is-with-us".'*

(Isaiah 7:14)

Nothing would ever be quite the same again once the
baby was born. An entirely new and unpredictable stage of
our lives had begun, which was to bring difficulties,
decisions, heartaches and great joy. This new presence in
our lives would, from this day forward, be with us in every
moment, waking and sleeping, and would change our lives
irreversibly. You, too, come silently into our hearts when
the time is right, changing us at our roots. Once you have
become God-with-us, we can never again be without you.

December 25th

*'Today in the town of David a saviour has been born
to you; he is Christ the Lord. And here is a sign for
you: you will find a baby wrapped in swaddling
clothes and lying in a manger.'*

(Luke 2:11–12)

We wrap our gifts in glittering paper and adorn them with
ribbons, hoping to make what is really very ordinary look
like something special. Your gift to us, your incarnate
Word, comes barely wrapped at all. You give us that which
is utterly special, but you wrap it in ordinariness, so that we
won't be afraid to receive it.

December 26th

*'Happy the eyes that see what you see, for I tell
you that many prophets and kings wanted to see
what you see and never saw it; to hear what you hear,
and never heard it.'*

(Luke 10:23–24)

When we catch a glimpse of you in a baby's first grasp or
an old man's memories, in the first crocus or the last
autumn rose, we see what no book contains nor human
wisdom can reveal.

*The angel of the Lord appeared to Joseph in a dream
and said: 'Get up, take the child and his mother with
you, and escape into Egypt, and stay there until I tell
you, because Herod intends to search for the child and
do away with him.'*

(Matthew 2:13–14)

'Where's the baby Jesus?' little Paul asked his parents, his
voice full of disbelief, as he gazed at the crib in the church
on Christmas morning. The day passed; dinner was over,
the new games had been played, and evening came. The
family watched the television news. '*There's* the baby Jesus!'
exclaimed Paul with conviction, pointing to the pictures
of a refugee family fleeing with their baby, the sound of
gunfire at their heels.

December 28th

When they had done everything the Law of the Lord required, they went back to Galilee, to their own town of Nazareth. Meanwhile the child grew to maturity, and he was filled with wisdom and God's favour was with him.

(Luke 2:39–40)

It is not enough simply to do what your Law commands us. You ask us not merely to obey, but to *grow*.

December 29th

*The moonlight will be bright as sunlight and
sunlight itself will be seven times brighter – like the
light of seven days in one – on the day the Lord
dresses the wound of his people and heals
the bruises his blows have dealt.*

(Isaiah 30:26)

In your hands we see the silver gleam of the surgeon's
knife, cutting the cancers from our hearts, but in your eyes
we see the golden light of a healer's love, releasing us from
pain into wholeness.

December 30th

We have all withered like leaves
and our sins blew us away like the wind.

(Isaiah 64:6)

Out in the garden the fallen leaves settle like a blanket over the withered grass. It looks as desolate as my own storm-swept heart so often feels, yet I know that this blanket of fallen-ness is covering and sheltering the unborn seeds of springtime.

December 31st

Let the heavens rejoice and earth be glad
let the sea and all within it thunder praise.
Let the land and all it bears rejoice,
all the trees of the wood shout for joy
at the presence of the Lord for he comes,
he comes to rule the earth.

(Psalm 96:11–13)

In the last hours of the dying year our hearts and our homes break out in celebration, to welcome the new. The winter trees are gestating the coming springtime and you, Lord, are growing us into the fullness of our eternal destiny in you.